Indians of Arizona

Indians of Arizona

of

A Contemporary Perspective

Thomas Weaver, *Editor*

Emil W. Haury	Bernard L. Fontana
Gordon V. Krutz	Emory Sekaquaptewa
Frank Lobo	Barry Bainton

Ruth Hughes Gartell

The University of Arizona Press

Tucson, Arizona

Photos courtesy
Arizona State Museum,
University of Arizona,
primarily by *Helga Teiwes-French.*

Figs. 3.1 and 3.2 — *Bureau of American Ethnology,*
and Fig. 2.6 — *Tad Nichols.*

THE UNIVERSITY OF ARIZONA PRESS

Third printing 1979

Contents

TABLES

MAPS

ILLUSTRATIONS

Preface

INDIANS HAVE BEEN PART of the mythology and world view of Americans throughout the history of the United States. They have played an important part in the formation of our literature, theatre, and fine arts. Many of our foods, place names and other cultural elements derive directly from Indians of North America. It is surprising, in view of the eminent position held by the Indian in our culture and history, that so many false notions and misunderstandings are held regarding Indians. This is particularly surprising in Arizona, in view of the greater visibility and cultural impact of such a large proportion of the population.

The chapters in this book try to answer the following commonly asked questions:

Who is an Indian?

How many Indians live in Arizona?

Where do they live?

How much land do they control?

Where do Indians come from?

How different are they from one another?

What has been the history of the relations between Indians and non-Indians?

What is the relationship of the Indian to the State of Arizona? To the federal government?

What services are provided for Indians by the state and federal governments?

What is the legal status of Indians? How are they governed? Can they be taxed?

Can a non-Indian do business on an Indian reservation? Is the non-Indian subject to tribal courts? Can Indians be sued for failure to fulfill a contract?

Under what conditions do Indians live today? Are Indians as poor as we hear? What do Indians do to help themselves? What kind of work can they do? What do Indians contribute to the Arizona economy? What is the economic potential of Indian human and land resources?

Have Indians been cheated out of their lands and natural resources? What protection do they have under state and federal laws? Are Indians citizens? Can they vote? Can they drink alcoholic beverages?

What is their level of educational achievement? What kinds of schools do Indians attend? Who pays for these schools? Does the state receive money from the federal government to educate Indians?

What will happen to Arizona Indians in the future?

This book was originally produced by members of the Department of Anthropology, the Arizona State Museum, and the Bureau of Ethnic Research of the University of Arizona for the Arizona Academy's Annual Town Hall meeting, held April 18-21, 1971. Used in the discussion of the relationship of the state's agencies to its Indian citizens, the report has been both revised and expanded for widespread general use.

Individuals identified with the collaborative preparation were as follows: Raymond H. Thompson, head of the Department of Anthropology and director of the Arizona State Museum, was director for the academy project. Thomas Weaver, director of the Bureau of Ethnic Research, served as research team coordinator and editor. Other members were Bernard L. Fontana, museum ethnologist; Emory Sekaquaptewa, attorney and assistant coordinator of Indian programs; Gordon Krutz, coordinator of Indian programs; and Ruth Hughes Gartell, Frank Lobo, and Barry Bainton, research associates. We are especially grateful for typing the various drafts of this report to the following secretaries in the Bureau of Ethnic Research and the Department of Anthropology: Mrs. Billie Brewer, Mrs. Jan Hastings, Mrs. Chris Mathis, Miss Josephine Cento, Miss Grace Leal, and Miss Beverly Modory. Research assistance was provided by Scott Rushford and Peteris Dajevskis, and photographs by Helga Teiwes-French, Arizona State Museum. We appreciate the assistance of the University of Arizona Press in effecting publication under its imprint.

Finally, we wish to acknowledge a grant from the Doris Duke American Indian Oral History Project of The University of Arizona which made possible the collecting of data on urban Indians in the state (chapter 6).

1. The Arizona Indian in Perspective

Thomas Weaver and Gordon Krutz

THE ARIZONA INDIAN is a product of a multi-cultural past. His behavior, as anyone else's, is the result of past influences which have been modified by his immediate social surroundings. Regardless of the origins of modifications — some have been imposed upon the Indian, others he has chosen for himself — the cultures of the various Indian groups are continually changing.

If the reader could transport himself back to 10,000 B.C. in the territory we now know as Arizona, he would find different peoples following different cultural patterns. In that early time these people were hunters of large game and later hunters of small animals and gatherers of wild plants and fruits. Around 300 B.C. a new group of migrants came to the central Gila River Valley bringing the rudiments of what was to become an agricultural tradition. Although these cultures were unusually advanced — excavated irrigation systems, refined farming implements and weapons give credence to this level of achievement — these early people would not be like our contemporary Indians. And the same can be said about the raiding Apaches who followed the farmers into Arizona in the sixteenth century.

What happened to these people? What happened to their cultures? Their descendants are still living in Arizona, but truly they are not the same Indians nor are they following the same living patterns.

The Indians were changed by those new arrivals with whom they came into contact — the Spanish conquistadores, and Mormon and other settlers from white America to the east. Some Indian cultures changed more rapidly than others, but they all did change.

The misconception still exists in some circles that since Indians no longer have an aboriginal culture to look to for guidance, they must pattern their behavior after the dominant white value system. But the fact is that the Indian does have a culture which is different not only from their traditional but from the modern white culture, as well. The Indian can no more be reproved for failing to be inculcated with white rules, norms of behavior, ambitions and expectations, than can the non-Indian for his failure to assimilate the earliest culture of the region, that of the Indian.

What may be the first step in many cases in understanding the Indians of Arizona is the refutation of the many commonly held stereotypes about Indians in general.

When the Spaniards arrived in the early seventeenth century, they found the entire region inhabited by many groups of Indians. Some were town-dwelling farmers, many were seminomadic hunters and raiders, and some lived in small bands of hunters and gatherers. The period of Spanish and Mexican influence lasted until the takeover of Arizona by the United States in 1854.

American intervention took the form of isolating Indians on reservations, using schools to force the assimilation of Indian youth into a non-Indian mold, and after 1887, introducing to some reservations the idea of individual ownership of land. Treaty making with the Indians came to a halt in the late nineteenth century, coupled with a hiatus in a relationship of mutual consent.

The first three decades of the twentieth century saw the growth of the Bureau of Indian Affairs and its increasing involvement in the lives of Indians. More reservations were created in Arizona, and in 1924 United States citizenship was bestowed on all Indians who qualified on the same terms as other citizens.

The "New Deal" for Indians was marked by the passage in 1934 of the Indian Reorganization Act and the reinstitution of working out solutions to problems through bilateral agreements between Indians and the United States government. All Arizona tribes except the Navajo adopted constitutions and formed governing bodies under the provisions of the Indian Reorganization Act. The Johnson-O'Malley Act, passed in the same year, provided federal support for Indian education in public schools. Reservation schools continued to be operated by the Bureau of Indian Affairs or by missionaries.

Federal Indian policy in the post World War II era shifted from attempts to revitalize tribal structures to forceful efforts to terminate the special relationships between Indians and the United States. Although it is legally possible for Arizona under federal statute to extend civil and criminal jurisdiction over its Indian reservations — provided the Indians consent — it has thus far shown no inclination to do so.

There are various definitions of Indians, but self-identification seems to be the best criteria. Arizona Indians numbered approximately 83,000 in 1960. With new criteria based primarily on self-identification, the 1970 U.S. Census identified closer to 100,000 Indians in Arizona. With the possible exception of California with its large number of relocated Indians, this figure makes Arizona one of the states with the largest number of Indians.

Indians live on 26 percent of Arizona's land, while approximately 20 percent reside in urban areas. This urban population is most neglected because of its lack of visibility — lost in the midst of many more people of other ethnic backgrounds. But the urban Indian's problems are greater by far than those of his friends and enemies in the city. Usually poorly educated, poorly trained, he comes to the city with two strikes against him. He is part of the city because he lives there, but he is still also part of the reservation because of his frequent visits and his many ties there.

Indians in Arizona are struggling for economic and political independence, but, except for some reservations, they are still very much under the jurisdiction and domination of the Bureau of Indian Affairs. Laws have been enacted by Congress which compensate the state for assuming greater and greater responsibility for its Indian citizens. These services, which parallel those provided for non-Indians, undoubtedly will be extremely helpful to Arizona's Indians.

Arizona Indian tribal governments exercise inherent and sovereign powers, although this sovereignty is limited by treaties, statutes, and agreements made with the government of the United States. Tribal governments are constitutionally organized, except for the Navajo, and are democratic in form. They are like municipalities in character, and in some instances, they exercise specific powers conferred by Congress in addition to their inherent powers. They are also under administrative supervision of the federal government through the Bureau of Indian Affairs, but in theory, this supervision is limited to the extent of the federal government's right and power to control the affairs of Indians. This supervision has developed into a trust relationship in which the government acts as a guardian exercising trusteeship over its Indian wards. The fundamental principle with respect to state power over Indians is that Congress has preempted this field, so that states may act only where specifically given authority by Congress.

It is an interesting paradox that a once self-sustaining and healthy population should find itself living under poor conditions in a land of plenty. As an independent population, Arizona Indians, historically, made whatever political, migratory, and cultural adjustments necessary to maintain proper diet and shelter. Today, despite the many innovative programs available for improvement, only 16 percent of the Arizona

Indian population has adequate housing. Water and sanitary conditions match the poor condition of the homes.

Tuberculosis and hepatitis occur more than 7½ times, streptococcus infections more than 34 times, and rheumatic fever almost 119 times more frequently among the Navajo than in the general U.S. population. Figures and rates are comparable among other Indian groups in the state and with other diseases as well. Malnutrition among Indian children is a commonplace occurrence. Because new programs have been in effect only since the early 1960s, it is too soon to evaluate their impact. But judging from the past results of similar, although less widely spread efforts, pessimism and cynicism will continue to prevail.

Although unemployment indices continue at a high level for Indians, not to mention the large numbers of people left out of these statistics because they are "unemployable" or have been out of the labor force for long periods of time, a new day seems to be dawning for self-sufficiency and self-determination in the development of reservation economics. Many more new programs and opportunities are available to Indians than ever before, and Indians apparently are beginning to take advantage of their long dormant human and natural resources.

The American Indian is subjected to an educational system which is the product of a long historical process. Indians are one of the most poorly trained and poorly educated groups in Arizona. The average dropout rate for Indian children is 37 percent, ranging from 15 to 60 percent. A majority of Indian students are behind in grade as measured by age. Education has been one of the principal battlegrounds for cultural conflict between the Indian and European-American. The problems facing Indian education today derive from the many attempts of European-Americans to assimilate the Indian into the culture of the dominant society. The structure of the present educational system may provide a solution to these problems, but the shortcomings of previous educational policies must be recognized and more attention must be paid to the cultural factors that have contributed to the present plight of Indian education.

The perspectives provided in this book reveal the results of a long series of injustices in Indian-white relationships. From the broader viewpoint, injustice can be viewed as a two-way affair. For the Indian, injustice is seen as losing much of his aboriginal territory, being placed in a dependency role, and having a set of values superimposed with no consideration for his desires. From a different perspective, injustice can be viewed as the limitation for economic development of an area through the placing of millions of acres in federal trust status, removing land from the state's tax rolls, and placing the burden of support on the non-Indian population. The term injustice would, of course, depend upon a perspective related to one's primary goals. Injustice, then, results from conflicts of interest and human misunderstanding oftentimes aggravated through individual application or inapplication of institutional laws. These laws may be unjust and place further stress on good relationships. Examples are the refusal to accept American Indians as citizens until 1924, or the denial of the right to purchase liquor until 1953.

Today, we continue to see social injustices in Indian-white relationships, encouraged through stereotyping of Indians by the dominant society, and especially through television and the movies.

The stereotype of the American Indian thus presented is of a warrior of the Plains culture type, who wears elaborate feathered war bonnets, lives in teepees, rides horses, is prone to violence, tortures and scalps his victims, yells a lot when attacking a fort, does war dances, and is highly nomadic. Television viewers are only recently beginning to realize that the native Indian "language" is not a heavily accented and ungrammatical English, but what the viewer does not yet realize is that there are over six major linguistic stocks in North America with nearly three hundred languages, and that no two Indian cultures are alike. The image of the Indian created by the communications media is a personal affront to the Indian and frequently places stress on the Indian-white relationship.

More dangerous to this relationship is an image resulting from direct social contact in which the white population, although realizing that there are differences between tribal groups, may persistently view the Indian as undependable, immoral, apathetic, and ignorant — one who sits by while his children drop out of school and is content to hold menial and sporadic employment. Because of his increasing demands for welfare and his failure to carry his share of property taxes, he is considered a burden to society. He is considered immoral because he practices non-Christian ceremonies, and apathetic because he seems to accept willingly the status quo without attempting to improve his position.

On the other hand, the Indian views the white population as rude, inconsistent, immoral, wasteful, destructive, and without heart. The white man is rude because he is impatient and too direct in his relationships with other people, and rudeness is associated with a violation of rules of etiquette which condition Indian behavior. Whites are inconsistent because their Indian policy has reversed itself at least four times since the 1890s, and more frequently because their reservation policies may change with each new superintendent. Because the white man says one thing and practices another, he is immoral. The Indian recognizes the dual standards of religious norm and behavior found in business relations and the serial polygamy practiced through temporary marriages. He feels it is immoral not to look after the aged and needy who instead are referred to agencies. Because he has wasted millions of acres of sacred land through the plow and the saw, destroyed wildlife, polluted streams and rivers, and contaminated the air, the white man is wasteful and destructive. Finally, the white man is without heart since he places a greater value on economic achievement than he does on human relationships and spiritual development.

Justice, then, could be a more harmonious relationship between the Indian and the dominant society — a relationship in which Indians are given the right to determine their fate without intervention, in which their children are helped rather than discriminated against because of differences in behavior and speech, in which employers recognize the Indian's cultural needs in religious ceremonial participation, and in which members of the dominant society attempt to learn from the Indian ideals of close family life, group achievement, and a more harmonious relationship with nature.

2. Before History

Emil W. Haury

THE NATURAL FORCES that shaped the Arizona landscape in geologic times also left a subtle imprint upon the lives of its present-day inhabitants. This is evident in the occupations of the people — in mining, cattle growing, arid land agriculture, tourism, and even in the out-of-doors homelife and forms of recreation. The influences of environment were just as emphatically stamped upon the lives of the native people who preceded our modern society by fifteen millennia. It is with this range of time that the archaeologist deals.

Archaeologists generally speak of large segments of the American continents as archaeological areas within which ancient societies developed and shared common ways of life. The Southwest is one of these areas, and the state of Arizona and most of New Mexico constitute its core. Parts of adjacent states to the north, west, and south are also included in this particular area (Fig. 2.1).

Three Geographic Zones

The story of man's adjustment to his environment begins with geography. Three startlingly different zones are evident in Arizona. From south to north, these are first, the flatlands of the desert, extending from sea level to almost three thousand feet, excluding the crests of the mountain ranges. Blessed with abundant arable land, but deprived by altitude and limiting precipitation factors, this land supports little more than thorny trees, brush, and cactus. Except for a few streams and springs, surface water is scarce.

Second, diagonally from the northwest to the southeast through the state stretches a mountainous belt with an altitude varying from the upper

---

This chapter originally appeared in *Arizona: Its People and Resources,* 2d ed. rev. (Tucson: University of Arizona Press, 1972), pp. 17-27.

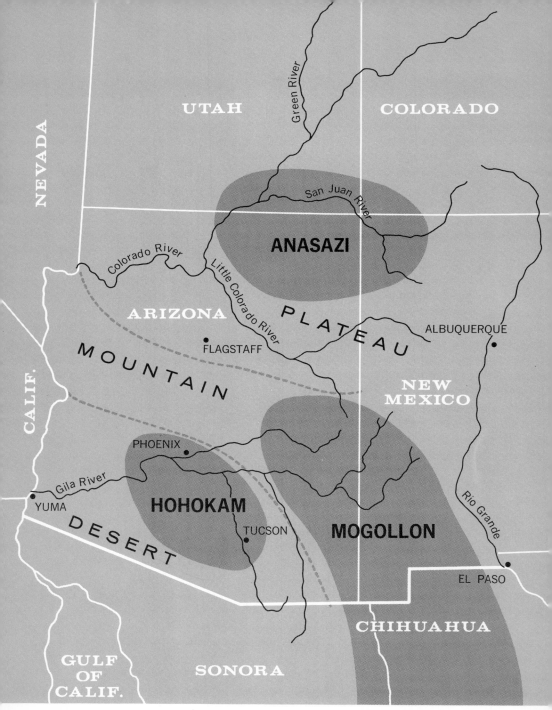

Fig. 2.1 Approximate location of the three principal culture centers in about A.D. 700.

desert limits to twelve thousand feet. Surface water is abundant, stemming from generous rainfall. Forests and grass cover the area, but good farming acreage is sparse.

The third zone is the northern plateau with an elevation of about one mile. Much of this region is barren upland, but it includes vast stretches of juniper and piñon. It is studded with colorful mesas and cut by intricate networks of canyons. Although very beautiful, the area lacks water and productive soil, two ingredients essential to prosperous living.

Each of these three land types supported and nurtured native populations before the European conquest. Nature imposed restrictions upon what could be done by a people solely dependent upon the resources of the land. Thus, to a marked extent, uniform human cultures arose in each of these zones. The sharp boundaries separating their territories disappeared only after each group had mastered its local environment. Once that was done, migrations from zone to zone began.

Ancient Tribes

Within the time limits of the Christian Era, therefore, the archaeologist recognizes the rise of three principal old tribal entities who left, in the wake of their decline and fall, hundreds of ruins broadcast over the Arizona landscape. Each distinct tribe centered in one of the three geographical areas.

Because these societies left no records from which the archaeologist can name them, the archaeologist has classified them arbitrarily. Beyond the Mogollon Rim, the northern uplands, or the Colorado Plateau, contained the Anasazi (Basketmaker-Pueblo) culture. Anasazi is a Navajo word meaning "The Ancient Ones." The Navajo Indians, recent immigrants into the Southwest, use this word when they speak of those who built and left the ruins on the lands which they now occupy.

The Mogollon people centered in the mountain belt, particularly in the eastern half. Not knowing what these people called themselves, archaeologists found it fitting to apply to them the name of an early Spanish general, also given to the Mogollon Rim in Arizona and Mogollon Mountains in New Mexico.

In the south, the earliest inhabitants of the desert area are called Hohokam, a word borrowed from the Pima language meaning "All Used Up."

Several other groups in the northwestern quarter of Arizona have been identified by archaeologists, for example, the Patayan and Sinagua.

But they were of minor importance when compared with the three major ancient peoples.

Man's Arrival in Arizona

No one knows when man first set foot in Arizona. By conservative reckoning, this was from twelve thousand to fifteen thousand years ago. As archaeologists better understand the evidence they accumulate and study, this estimate for man's arrival may be pushed back in time. It is certain that the earliest Arizonans must claim kinship with the enormous reservoir of humanity in Asia. It is reasonably certain that they were attracted to this part of the world by the abundance of big game upon which their lives at that time depended — the elephants, camels, horses, sloths, and bison that lived in another geologic era. These first people were hunters, on the move, a simple folk, leaving behind only occasional traces of their presence in campsites and in the remains of animals killed with their primitive weapons.

The bones of an elephant (Columbian Mammoth), with eight spear points in the head and rib cage, mutely evidence the hunting skill of this early man. These remains were discovered imbedded deeply in the earth along Greenbush Creek near Naco, Arizona. At the Lehner ranch near Hereford, in the San Pedro River valley, big game hunting was common. Here were found the bones of nine pachyderms, several horses, bison, and tapir, slaughtered around a water hole in a fossil stream. Spear points and stone butchering tools were uncovered at the same site. Even the remains of two fires upon which some of these animals may have been roasted were discovered. With the aid of skills developed by the geologist and the atomic physicist, particularly the use of carbon dating, the age of the events described above has been dated back at least eleven thousand years.

Evidence of these early inhabitants has also been found in Ventana Cave on the Papago Indian Reservation, one hundred miles west of Tucson. Sundry stone tools, scattered bones of a variety of extinct animals, and charcoal from their fires have been unearthed beneath fifteen feet of refuse — the accumulation of centuries of debris left by later occupants.

These archaeological discoveries illuminate the first chapter of Arizona's history. They are preserved in the excellent exhibits of the Arizona State Museum on the campus of the University of Arizona.

What we know of man in Arizona from this point on is related to the disappearance of the animals upon which he subsisted. The climate, fauna, and flora of those days were much different. With the glacial retreat of the last Ice Age came the end of big game. But man's hunting skill also hastened the doom of the animal herds. When man was deprived of his primary food source, he was forced to adjust to other foods or to perish.

The Cochise

The Cochise people form the next connecting link in man's early history. Their record stretches over at least eight thousand years. Temporally, they are sandwiched between the elephant hunters and the more highly developed people of the Christian Era. Archaeologists have named these people after Cochise County, where many traces of them were first found in the alluvial valley deposits brought to view by the heavy arroyo cutting which began in the last decades of the nineteenth century.

While the earliest of these Cochise people knew and hunted the extinct animals, the loss of the big game forced them to turn to smaller quarry, the species of animals we know today. They also turned to a greater dependence upon plant foods. Thus, they became gatherers primarily, demonstrating their capacity to adjust to a changing environment. They developed appropriate stone tools for collecting and preparing vegetal foods. Campsites of this period have produced large quantities of such tools. Among these, and undoubtedly the most important, was the functionally related pair of grinding stones consisting of the nether stationary unit against whose surface the movable hand-held stone was operated. This was the prototype of the mano and metate associated with the farming societies of later times.

Until approximately 2000 B.C., the Cochise people collected foods provided by nature. At that time, or thereabouts, a cereal grain in the early stages of domestication came to them by way of the people in Mexico. This grain was a primitive form of corn, or maize, in which each kernel was separately sheathed in a husk and attached to a small cob. The introduction of this new food changed man into a planter and food producer, for corn does not reseed itself, but must be planted and tended. This was a revolution of major proportion in Southwestern culture history. To some extent, man could now begin to control his environment. He could produce more than he could consume. But the capacity to store the surplus food was essential to the success of the system. It took some time for the widespread adoption of corn, but by the beginning of the Christian Era, most of the people in the Southwest were well on their way to a sedentary agricultural life.

About this time, two other vegetal plants, squash and beans, were introduced to enrich and stabilize the economy. It is at this point that archaeologists begin to use the regional tribal distinctions associated with the three physiographic provinces of Arizona. The respective histories of these three tribal groups can be traced through their artifacts with increasing reliability and completeness to the present.

The Hohokam, the Mogollon, and the Anasazi experienced special problems in dealing with their environments — the desert, the mountain zone, and the plateau, respectively. But of these problems, water was primary. It was difficult to know where to find it, and how to use and control it for the benefit of all. A second major problem was obtaining food, both in collection and in production. These early peoples had to coax crops from an unyielding soil and were handicapped by contrary elements of nature. A third difficulty was found in living from day to day. They were forced to develop smoothly operating social, political, and religious systems. While the three groups shared numerous traits, their differences distinguished them from one another. Although the specific origins of the Anasazi and Mogollon are unknown, their roots dip back into the culture of old Cochise people. The Hohokam were believed to have been immigrants from Mexico several centuries before the time of Christ. All were stimulated to adopt higher living standards by the introduction of new crops, new agricultural practices, and new arts, such as pottery making, from the more highly developed cultures of Mexico.

The Hohokam

It was the Hohokam who built the irrigation canals that drew water from living streams, diverting it to thirsty fields far distant from the source. Several hundred miles of such engineering projects have been traced in the Salt and Gila river valleys. Some of those canals match modern ones in size. In fact, in pioneering days, a few of the Hohokam ditches were restored to use by cleaning them out, patching breaks in the banks, and turning water into them. No Indian achievement north of Mexico, in pre-Conquest times, surpasses the Hohokam canal system for planning, expenditure of effort, and for the evident inter-community organization that produced it. They were master-farmers, producing corn, beans, squash, and cotton in an arid land by irrigation and water control. Some form of canal irrigation may have existed by 300 B.C., but the system reached its height between 1000 and 1400.

By developing such an intricate system of canals, the Hohokam accomplished another important objective: they had freedom of choice for the location of their villages. Ordinarily the village or town site was picked because of the existence of natural water. But canals, going far

Fig. 2.2 Fourteenth-century irrigation canal was part of early Hohokam engineering project.

from streams, opened new possibilities of mobility and location — the kind of emancipation from the environment achieved in modern society often only by digging wells. The classic example of this mobility of location, dating from the canal period, was the large settlement of Los Muertos, six miles south of Tempe, excavated by Frank Hamilton Cushing in 1887–88. There, hundreds of people lived in the desert, six miles from the Salt River, sustained by the thin lifeline of a canal. No other prehistoric people in the Southwest matched this feat. From this fact the archaeologist deduces the existence of a political and social organization that had community welfare at heart.

Some of the desert dwellers, such as those living on what was later the Papago Reservation, were not fortunate enough to have access to live streams. Here control of the surface runoff was the key to successful living. Gathering ditches were one answer. One of these ran in a westerly direction for nearly ten miles from the base of Baboquivari Peak. It cut across numerous small natural drainages on the gentle piedmont slope, collecting the rain water and directing it to fertile ground in the lowland. This was a precarious form of irrigation, but it must have worked at least much of the time.

The discovery that irrigated agriculture was practiced in Mexico during the first millenium B.C. has helped modern archaeologists to understand what happened in the valleys of the Gila and Salt rivers. The Hohokam learned the art of irrigation from their kinsmen in Mexico. It was Hohokam genius, however, that modified the principles they knew to meet the demands of the local environment. To many people, the Hohokam, more than any other group of prehistoric Southwesterners, exemplify man's capacity to rise to the challenge of a harsh environment by understanding it and turning its hidden advantages to his favor, thereby setting the stage for the development of what we choose to call civilization.

As it did on all other farming people, the miracle of agriculture left a deep imprint on Hohokam society. The growing season of plants, and labor investments in canals and fields, anchored the people to the soil. This meant permanent villages in which the labors of a few could produce food for many. Food surpluses permitted the release of time and energy for other pursuits which contributed to the advance of Hohokam culture.

Impressive and solidly constructed domestic and religious architecture was not among the great Hohokam achievements. For more than a thousand years the family home was a roofed-over pit in the ground, looking like an earthen mound from the outside. With a side entrance, the inside was comfortable in both summer and winter, an efficient shade in spite of its simplicity. Until the 1950s, archaeologists had not found any architectural remains that might have been used primarily for religious observances. The kiva, either large or small, a common feature in Mogollon and Anasazi ruins, was apparently entirely lacking. But in 1958, scientists from the Arizona State Museum cleared the debris away from an earthen mound situated near Gila Bend, disclosing a flat-topped, pyramidal temple base. The age of this structure was close to A.D. 1100, and it is one of the many links that relate the Hohokam to the high civilizations of central Mexico.

Another prominent feature in some Hohokam sites is the ball court, in which the Indians played a game doubtless similar to that for which the stone-walled courts found in Toltec and Maya ruins were used. An old ball made of native rubber, found in a pottery jar near Casa Grande, hints that balls of this kind were used in the game. As in Mexico, there were probably religious aspects to the game, but of these nothing is known. The evidence suggests that the ball game was played in special arenas as early as A.D. 700 and that the custom persisted at least until 1400. During this period there was a reduction in the length of the court and a shift in orientation from east-west to north-south. It is probable that the kickball races of the Pima and Papago Indians represent a faint echo and survival of the early formalized game.

Fig. 2.3   Snaketown archaeologists found housefloors
revealing a thousand years of architectural history.

Fig. 2.4   Pottery of the Hohokam is distinguished by
its shapes, designs, and red-on-buff color.

The effect of a sedentary farming life on the Hohokam is best seen
in their arts and crafts. As the original Arizona cotton growers, a plant
that came to them from Mexico perhaps before A.D. 300, the Hohokam
also became producers of fine textiles. The unfortunate custom of cremating the dead with their finery has destroyed many of the products of
the loom, but scraps have survived in a few rock shelters, such as Ventana
Cave, where the Hohokam once lived. From these scraps it is evident
that, in addition to the simple weaving of cloth, a number of complicated
techniques were used. Tapestry, twill, gauze, and an ingenious lace-like
cloth known as weft-warp openwork provided means for decorating cloth.
Evidence of these is found among the neighbors of the Hohokam to the
north and east, who obviously were inspired by Hohokam achievement,
and many of whom were almost certainly supplied with raw cotton from
Hohokam fields through trade.

In terms of quality, Hohokam pottery was not of the best. But what.
it lacked in quality of body it made up for in form and design. Shapes
run a wide gamut from the conventional to the eccentric (Fig. 2.4) and
some of these, such as the legged vessels, also suggest affinities with the
people of Mexico. The buff-colored pottery was painted with a red-brown
iron oxide pigment, producing what the archaeologist calls red-on-buff of
various kinds. This pottery is readily distinguishable from that of other

Southwestern people. Most characteristic of the designs were repeated
life forms which, with a few cursive brush strokes and without detail,
achieved an amazing degree of animation. Careful stratigraphic studies
at Snaketown on the Gila River Indian Reservation and in other ruins
have traced at least fifteen hundred years of Hohokam pottery history.

The Hohokam talent for modeling clay is best revealed in figurines
which usually copied the human form. The occurrence of many of these
with cremated dead suggests ritual use. In some instances it appears that
efforts were made to capture the personality of a real person.

Stone sculpture was also an outstanding Hohokam trait, best exemplified by slate palettes for mixing pigments and small receptacles with
bas-relief decoration. Sculpture was limited to small objects, differing in
this respect from the monumental works of the Mexican Indians.

Because the Hohokam were nearer to the sea than any other Southwestern Indians, they found sea shell to be a material which could readily
be fashioned into a large variety of ornaments. They excelled all Indians
north of Mexico in this art, and capitalized upon their ability to acquire
shell easily by trading it, both raw and shaped, to tribes far and near. Their
crowning achievement was the development of an etching technique,
whereby a pattern was obtained by immersing a shell painted with a wax
in an acid which was probably the fermented juice of the saguaro fruit

Fig. 2.5   Hohokam ornamented seashell with acid etching.

(Fig. 2.5). This technique was apparently unique to the Hohokam and was invented by them by A.D. 1100, some 400 years before the same principle was employed in Europe by craftsmen to decorate metal armor.

The custom of cremating the dead began in the Southwest long before the time of Christ. The incinerated bones of the deceased were generally enshrined in earthenware pots, sometimes with lavish accompaniments. Only those which resisted fire, such as objects of stone, bone, and shell survived, but fragments of cloth and other perishable objects are occasionally found among the ashes. The loss of these objects, as well as the destruction of the physical remains of the people by fire, has seriously limited the archaeologist's ability to write as fully as he would like about all the aspects of the Hohokam people and their culture.

Particularly important is the role the Hohokam played as the recipients and modifiers of the elements of high Mexican civilizations. Of all Southwestern people, they mirrored the achievements of Mexico most clearly, accepting what they wanted and changing it to fit their situation. The direct import of a few things, such as copper bells and pyrite-encrusted mosaic plaques, is evidence of trade contacts. Some archaeologists see the Hohokam as migrants from Mexico. They were unique among ancient Southwestern tribes in their effective adjustment to desert living and in their imaginative combining of native and imported ideas.

By A.D. 1400, the Hohokam went into an eclipse as a virile group. Throughout the Southwest, this was a period of drastic changes, which caused the decline of other groups as well as the Hohokam. Paradoxically, archaeologists at the beginning of the 1970s knew less about the period between A.D. 1400 and 1700 than about the culture history of the millenium before 1400, but there are reasons for believing that the Pima and Papago Indians are the modern descendants of the Hohokam.

The Mogollon

Standing in sharp contrast to the Hohokam were the mountain-dwelling Mogollon people. By comparison they were a drab people, their culture more difficult to define, their contributions to the total culture history of the Southwest undistinguished. They inhabited the Arizona-New Mexico border country south of the White Mountains, stretching down into Mexico for an undetermined distance (Fig. 2.1). While there is some dispute over the origin of the Mogollon, the evidence seems clear that their roots are in the Cochise culture. The mountains gave them ready access to water and plentiful game, but little land for farming save in a few favored localities. Like that of many forest inhabitants, their life was simple, a response to environmental limitations.

Yet they were among the earliest Southwestern people to grow corn and to make pottery. At first this was unpainted. Later, it was decorated with red-earth pigments on a brown base. Superficially this resembled the pottery of the Hohokam, a likeness born of the common inspiration for both traditions from Mexico, but tribal distinctiveness is disclosed by the difference in the method of manufacture and the surface treatment. The introduction of potterymaking may be dated to the second or third century B.C. long before the art was learned by the Anasazi, their neighbors to the north. Corn reached them somewhat earlier than this.

Mogollon villages consisted of loosely arranged clusters of houses, partly underground and partly above, entered by means of covered ramps leading to floor level from the east. The idea of building walls of stone was foreign to them until late in their history. In most villages a large pit structure, much larger than those designed for family living, has been found. This is believed to have been a building for community ceremonial use. It is a reminder that, despite a simple and rigorous existence, the social, political, and religious aspects of Mogollon life may have been complex.

The material goods of the culture not destroyed by time and soil were mostly rough tools of stone, tips for arrows, metates for grinding corn, thin rock slabs for tilling the soil, grooved mauls for work requiring heavy blows, small stone bowls for pulverizing pigments, and similar items. The Mogollon excelled at producing the tubular stone pipe, technically the most difficult to make. A few simple bone tools were also used, and gambling pieces of the same material reveal at least one of their diversions. They knew the art of basketry and in late times, after A.D. 700, they wore cloth of cotton, a fiber almost surely imported from the Hohokam.

The Mogollon Indian was of medium build and stature, with a round head, not greatly different from many modern Indians. He wore few, if any ornaments, though he may have painted his body to offset this lack. At death he was tightly folded and placed in a shallow pit and was rarely accorded the luxury of accompanying food containers or tools.

Since the northern frontier of the Mogollon touched on the Anasazi, and beyond the western boundary was the Hohokam domain, cultural blending was inevitable, especially because the Mogollon were a culturally impoverished lot and their neighbors were not. The net result of this was a submergence of the old simple Mogollon way of life, and the rise of a more complex society basically Anasazi, also tinged with Hohokam, in which a few old Mogollon elements were retained. Archaeologists are greatly interested in a cultural tranformation of this kind because it reveals some of the processes of change. Although the Mogollon left an undistinguished record, having given little to their neighbors but having received much more, they added special and challenging problems to the archaeological past. Their modern descendants, if any, have not been identified.

The Anasazi

On the plateau to the north of the Mogollon was the homeland of the Anasazi. These people are the best known of all of the prehistoric Southwesterners because archaeologists have studied their ruins for nearly a century and because, until recent years, most expeditions focused their attention on this tribe. Furthermore, the Anasazi have received prominence through the designation of many of their abandoned homes as national monuments.

Much of the plateau is arid, and vast stretches have neither arable land nor readily accessible surface water. These two factors determined the deployment of the population, and because of these the population density was spotty over the plateau, varying from great centers such as Black Mesa and the Hopi country, the White Mountains, Mesa Verde, the Chaco Canyon, to the sparsely inhabited Painted Desert. The diversified environment of the plateau required the development of specialized techniques before the land could be made to produce foodstuffs in sufficient quantities to support towns. The Anasazi rose to this challenge with an amazing degree of skill. The compelling requisites of water and soil determined the extent to which a community could expand, and expansion was the tribal pattern, demanded by defense, group activities in farming, and proper conduct of religious ceremonies.

The Four Corners country, where Arizona, New Mexico, Colorado, and Utah come together, is generally regarded as the heartland of the Anasazi, and it is here that their oldest remains are found. These date from about the beginning of the Christian Era. Prior to this time the Anasazi were probably a nomadic people, but the earliest archaeological evidence is from the time when they were just adopting agriculture. Within a few centuries their living pattern was established. Their permanent dwellings, in or out of caves, resembled those of the Hohokam and Mogollon; these were often clustered in loose village arrangements. The bow and arrow replaced the spear-thrower or *atl-atl,* and pottery-making and the bean were added to the culture. Skills of the artisan were developed in basketry, and in the creation of woven sandals and sashes. Even music made its appearance with the development of flutes. The dog was domesti-

Fig. 2.6 A typical Anasazi "apartment house" — White House Ruins, Canyon de Chelly.

cated. All this represents great progress by the Anasazi people in adaptation to and control over the environment.

Then started a long upward climb, the molding of a new way of life a thousand years in the making. These steps are traceable in the thousands of ruins that dot the plateau. The climax of Anasazi achievements was from about A.D. 1000 to 1400. This was the time when the homes were often built in caves widely scattered through the canyons creasing the plateau (Fig. 2.6). But infinitely more pueblos, as Anasazi towns are known, were built in the open because there simply were not enough caves to supply natural shelter for all. It is incorrect, therefore, to think of Anasazi people as cliff dwellers only. They established their residence wherever land and water permitted, and if a cave was available, so much the better.

Due to a method of dating which was developed on the University of Arizona campus, archaeologists have been able to speak of the age of Anasazi remains with a definiteness not possible for any other New World ruins. Dendrochronology, or the study of tree-rings, as applied to the ruins of the Southwest, was the brainchild of Dr. A. E. Douglass. The timbers that went into the Anasazi residences are the main sources for the raw data upon which this system depends. When the archaeologist is able to refer to past events in terms of dated decades, quarter or half centuries, rather than in the vagueness of a relative chronology lacking calendar years as we know them, half of the battle to interpret prehistory is won. The Anasazi story has been enormously enriched because of this method of studying the past.

With the mastery of agricultural techniques, food surpluses followed. The ability to store excess food in jars, baskets, and bins (even to the point of tiding the people over lean years) provided the stability that resulted in an expanding population, large communities, specialization in the arts, and, inferentially, increasing complexity in the social, religious, and political systems.

The evolution of pueblo architecture from simple beginnings was one of the finest accomplishments of the Anasazi. The joining of room to room whether of stone or adobe, and the stacking of rooms to a height of four or five stories was the Anasazi method for packing people into the least possible space. The reason for this crowding is not clear since there was no shortage of land. While most towns grew by accretion in response to the expanding population, a few of them show planning as though following an architect's design. The monotony of solid room blocks was broken by plazas, providing easier access to the rooms and good space

Fig. 2.7 The white background is characteristic of Anasazi pottery. These pieces date from about 600 to 1300.

for outdoor activities. The plazas of our oldest Western towns are surely traceable to this old Indian custom.

Another noteworthy architectural feature was the underground kiva with specialized furnishings. As in the modern pueblo Indian villages where kivas are in use today, the prehistoric kivas were probably owned by the male members of the clans, and were used both as club houses and for secret religious rites. The great kivas, as much as seventy feet in diameter and strongly roofed, were the most impressive buildings ever erected in the Southwest until the Conquest. They served the larger communities as a place where rites vital to the group as a whole, such as rain-producing ceremonies, were performed.

A familiar sight on all Anasazi ruins of this climax period are the numerous fragments of pottery. Much of this has black patterns on white backgrounds, the most distinctive of all Anasazi hallmarks (Fig. 2.7). Many other kinds are also present, such as multi-colored pottery and the rough-surfaced cooking and storing pottery known as corrugated. All of these have special significance to the archaeologist because the shapes, colors, and designs show differences from place to place and time to time.

Other arts also reached a high level of perfection. Textiles of cotton (Fig. 2.8), robes of feather cloth, sandals in a great variety of weaves,

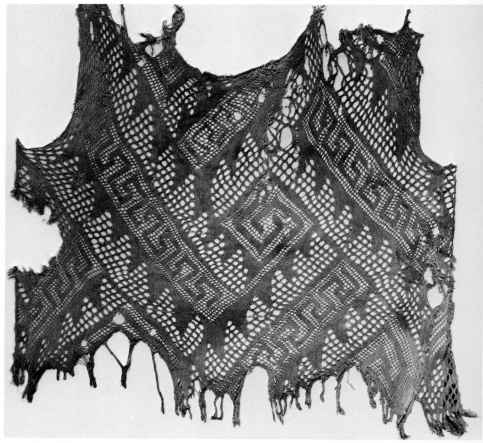

Fig. 2.8   A fourteenth-century cotton lace shirt from the Upper Tonto Cliff Ruin.

baskets, personal ornaments, ritual finery — all of these have been found by archaeologists.

The Anasazi dead were normally buried in the refuse heaps. From the graves come many of the objects that help archaeologists characterize the society. The skeletons reveal that these Indians have living descendants among such tribes as the Hopi, Zuñi, and the Rio Grande pueblos of New Mexico.

By A.D. 1400 some of the larger centers, thriving only one to two centuries before, had already been abandoned. The frontiers were shifting, mainly to the south out of the Four Corners country. The reasons for this still puzzle archaeologists. No satisfactory answer has yet been discovered, but it is certain that the causes were complex, interlocking, and that they influenced most of the Southwest.

This movement of people resulted in centers even larger than before, but far fewer in number. These enjoyed a brief spurt of cultural energy. By 1500, however, only the Hopi, Zuñi, and Rio Grande centers remained. Chroniclers of the Spanish Conquest, which began in 1540, record only seventy pueblo towns, and by then most of the old glory was lost. The number today stands at about twenty-six. Perhaps a factor in the concentration of the Anasazi during the fifteenth and sixteenth centuries was the arrival of wandering hunters, the Navajo and Apache Indians. Upsetting as their presence must have been, these nomads did no more than speed up the Anasazi decline; they did not initiate it.

Anasazi history, like that of the Hohokam, matches the worldwide pattern of the rise and fall of ancient societies. Though obscured by time, their achievements have lent drama to Arizona's past.

3. Historical Foundations

Bernard L. Fontana

ARIZONA'S ABORIGINAL POPULATION lived in the desert (Pima, Maricopa, Papago, Cocopa, Quechan, Mohave, and Chemehuevi), the mountains (Yavapai and Apache), and the plateau (Walapai, Havasupai, Hopi, Southern Paiute, and Navajo). Some of these people, the so-called Puebloans, practiced dry farming and lived in apartment-like houses clustered in villages. These are the Hopi Indians whose modern villages are Old Oraibi, New Oraibi (Kikotsmovi), Hotevilla, Bakabi, Shungopovi, Shipaulovi, Mishongovi, Sichomovi, Walpi, and Moenkopi. Another Arizona pueblo village is Hano, on the First Mesa of Hopiland, where Tewa-speaking immigrants settled next to the Hopis in the late seventeenth century. Polacca is a recent town with no political recognition as a village by the tribal council. Keams Canyon, headquarters for the Bureau of Indian Affairs' Hopi Indian Agency, is not a "pueblo" in any sense of the word, even though a great many Hopis live there. Begun as a trading post, it was laid out and built principally by non-Hopis.

Most Arizona Indians were what the Spaniards referred to as *rancheria* peoples. They lived in fixed settlements, farmed at least part of the time, and built their houses at a considerable distance from one another. Rancheria people frequently had more than one village, shifting from one settlement to another depending on the season of the year. These include the Pima and Papago Indians; the Yaqui Indians, who started arriving in Arizona late in the nineteenth century; the Havasupai, Walapai, and some of the Yavapai; and the Quechan (Yuma), Mohave, Maricopa, and Cocopa.

Arizona's Western Apaches and Navajos were organized into small, seminomadic bands. Although primarily hunters, gatherers and, in historic times, raiders, Navajos and Western Apaches did, in fact, farm. Western Apache groups and bands include the Eastern White Mountain and Western White Mountain bands of the White Mountain group; Carrizo, Cibecue proper, and Canyon Creek bands of the Cibecue group;

Fig. 3.1   A Papago brush house **(shaish ki)** in 1894, near Vamori, Arizona. This was the typical summer house until early in the twentieth century.

Pinal, Arivaipa, San Carlos proper, and Apache Peaks bands of the San Carlos group; the Mazatzal band and six semi-bands of the Southern Tonto group; and the Mormon Lake, Fossil Creek, Bald Mountain, and Oak Creek bands of the Northern Tonto group.

The first European settlers arriving in the area, which now includes Arizona, found a few bands of Indians who did not practice farming. These were hunting and gathering peoples who relied entirely upon wild produce for their food or upon trade or raiding among their agricultural neighbors. These included all three bands of the Chiricahua Apaches, most of whose descendants today live in New Mexico and Oklahoma; the westernmost group of Papago Indians, known as "Sobas" to the Spaniards and whose descendants may be represented in one or two families now living near Roll and Dome, Arizona; the Southern Paiute; the Chemehuevi; and the Southeastern Yavapai.

What is perhaps most important to remember with respect to Arizona's native groups is that they constituted communities which were generally self-reliant and independent and which wrested their living from local or regional resources.

Spain and Mexico: 1539-1854

The first Europeans to arrive in southern Arizona were neither its discoverers nor its first explorers. When the Franciscan priest, Marcos de Niza, rode into Arizona in 1539 with a large contingent of Spaniards in search of the fabled, if elusive, Seven Cities of Gold, they trod over well-worn trails. Marcos de Niza had been preceded in the region by at least twelve thousand years.

There were other sixteenth century adventurers who left their foreign footprints on Arizona soil: Coronado, the would-be colonizer; Antonio de Espejo, the Spanish prospector; and Juan de Oñate, who journeyed from his colony on the northern Rio Grande to the Lower Colorado River and back. Indeed, it was Oñate's colony in New Mexico, founded in 1598, which set the stage for 211 years of Spanish domination of New Mexico and the partial domination of Arizona for at least some of that time.

The first Europeans to explore the region of New Mexico and northern Arizona were Spaniards. Most of the first European colonists, soldiers and missionaries were from Spain and New Spain. Although many of the early Jesuit missionaries in southern Arizona were Italian, Swiss, Bavarian, Swede, Czech, German, and the like, they nonetheless owed an allegiance to Spain and were supported in their efforts by Spanish soldiers. And while the European settlement of New Mexico began in 1598 — not to mention earlier unsuccessful attempts — it was only after 1700 that the presence of Europeans was felt in the lives of most Arizona Indians, with the exception of Hopis, Navajos, and Apaches.

Spanish Influence

The European newcomers and their descendants left a lasting imprint on the native cultures of what in time was to become the state of Arizona. The Roman Catholicism which they brought with them has continued in various forms among many modern tribes; sheep, wool and silversmithing, still important to Navajo and Hopi Indians, are attributable directly to Hispanic introductions; the Spanish names of certain political positions, such as governor and lieutenant governor, are the names used today by the Pima. Many modern Indians still speak Spanish as a second language, although far more speak English instead. Virtually all Arizona Indian languages have Spanish loan words and many other Spanish language influences.

Several other traits found in contemporary Indian cultures were introduced by Spaniards and historical continuity can be demonstrated. Among these are such things as the hide drum used among Apaches and Hopis; the sun-baked adobe brick, still used for construction by the desert-dwelling tribes; beehive ovens; corner fireplaces; wheat, which in addition to native corn, is used in making several kinds of bread; certain games, such as cards, among Apaches; dances, such as the *matachine* dances of the Yaquis; and songs, especially hymns.

Although Spaniards introduced cattle, oxen, and horses into Arizona, their importance among modern Papagos, Apaches, and Walapais stems more from Anglo-American influence of the last half of the nineteenth century than from Spanish attempts to turn Indians into pastoralists. Only Navajos became true herders during the Spanish and Mexican periods. But Spanish influences cannot be gainsaid. Anglo-American "cowboy culture" has its roots in the plains of La Mancha and Estremadura in Spain.

Spanish Law

Curiously enough, Spanish law has had a profound effect on modern American Indian life. This is because the legal basis of the relationship between the United States government and American Indians has grown out of English international law and English international law owes its greatest debt to the Spanish jurist, Francisco de Vitoria. From Spain to England to the United States to the Indians of Arizona, Spanish law has left its mark on current events. The more straightforward attempts by Spaniards to influence permanently the legal and political institutions of these natives were less successful.

In spite of nearly two centuries of Spanish and Mexican influence on the Indians of Arizona, there is little question that the essential features of modern Indian life are more readily understood in terms of relatively recent history, the period of the Anglo-American contact. It is the Anglo-American heritage of modern Indian cultures, superimposed as it was on aboriginal and Spanish-modified traditions, that we have to take into account if we are to understand the present.

Fig. 3.2   The use of draft animals with wooden yoke of the type introduced by the Spaniards. This farmer and his cattle were photographed at Fresnal Village in 1894.

American Intervention

General Stephen Watts Kearny rode into Santa Fe, New Mexico, on August 18, 1846, at the head of some three hundred dragoons who made up his "Army of the West." He had come on behalf of the United States to take part in the war declared with Mexico a few months earlier. Securing Santa Fe without a fight, Kearny rode with his men across Arizona on the Gila Trail to California, still in 1846. The so-called "Treaty of Guadalupe Hidalgo," which officially ended the war with

Mexico, became law on July 4, 1848. In its wake, the United States had added most of what is now the state of New Mexico to her boundaries, along with all of Arizona north of the Gila River. The part of the state lying south of the Gila was lost to Mexico until the "Gadsden Purchase" of 1854.

Although General Kearny probably never thought of himself in the role, it was he who in fact became the vanguard of United States Indian policies in Arizona. His successful invasion of the region extended the traditions and laws of the United States over Indians in the area. Although each group of Indians has since had its own unique experience with Anglo-Americans, all aboriginal inhabitants share common experiences in the face of the United States' juggernaut of westward expansion. All, in due course, became subject to the same policies, regulations, and laws formulated largely in faraway Washington, D.C. These have left the Indians of Arizona with a portion of their common Anglo-American heritage.

By 1846 the great "Indian Removal" had about come to an end in which thousands of Indians living in the eastern United States had been relocated by force and cajolery west of the Mississippi River. Indian Territory as well as the United States was not large enough to accommodate more dislocated Indians. The discovery of gold in California led to the virtual settlement of the country by non-Indians from the Atlantic to the Pacific. America's aboriginal inhabitants were surrounded and slowly overwhelmed; all but the western tribes of Indians had been subdued. It was only on the western frontier, remote from the nation's centers of non-Indian population, that hostilities between whites and Indians remained a reality.

The first two-and-a-half decades of Indian affairs in Arizona were characterized by a lack of Indian removal; by the establishment of the reservation system which at once kept Indians out of the settlers' way and which protected at least a part of the Indians' aboriginal domains; by government attempts to train Indians on reservations in the various "arts of civilization," which is to say, to assimilate them while keeping them segregated; and by warfare with Navajos, Apaches, Yavapais, and to a lesser extent, Walapais. Engagements with Mohaves, Quechans, and Chemehuevis were rare skirmishes. Pimas, Papagos, Hopis, Maricopas, Cocopahs, Havasupais, and Kaibab Paiutes struggled against the Anglo-American invasion almost not at all. The Navajos were militarily defeated in 1864; the Walapais in 1869; the Yavapais in 1875; Western Apaches in 1881; and the Chiricahua Apaches, the last to capitulate, in 1886.

Reservations

The Legal Bases of Reservations

Under Spain and Mexico there had been no reservations in Arizona. But Anglo-Americans, who had adopted from England the policy of treating Indian tribes as if they were foreign powers, quickly applied concepts of the post-Indian Removal era to this newly-won land. The official position of the United States in law, based upon an 1823 Supreme Court decision was that

> . . . discovery [by Europeans] gave an exclusive right to extinguish the Indian title of occupancy, either by purchase or by conquest . . . The existence of this power [of the Government of the United States to grant lands] must negative [sic] the existence of any right which may conflict with, and control it. An absolute title to lands can not exist, at the same time, in different persons, or in different governments . . . Indian inhabitants are to be considered merely as occupants, to be protected, indeed, while in peace, in possession of their lands, but to be deemed incapable of transferring the absolute title to others.

It is thus that only the United States could, did, and can set aside lands from the public domain for the benefit of particular groups of Indians. As "conventional arrangements," Indian reservations were nothing new in United States policy. Even before there had been a United States the English had created reserves for Indian use and occupancy along the Atlantic coast. As early as 1653 the English assigned tribesmen of the Powhatan Confederacy to reservations in Tidewater, Virginia, thus effectively segregating them from non-Indian culture.

When the Territory of New Mexico, which included Arizona until 1863, was officially created by the Act of September 9, 1850, the Department of Indian Affairs (as the Bureau of Indian Affairs was called) had the year before been transferred from the War Department to the Department of the Interior. One of the first commissioners of Indian affairs to serve under the secretary of the interior, George W. Manypenny (1853-1857), determined that Indian removal must cease and that the United States must write a new code of regulations with respect to the management of Indian affairs. When Manypenny argued that "conventional arrangements" be made for Arizona's Indians, he was not calling for their removal or annihilation. He was urging that lands be reserved for Indian use.

It was only after the United States acquired southern Arizona in 1854 that attention was paid to any of Arizona's Indians other than the Navajos. An Indian agent, a political appointee as all agents were, named John Walker was sent to Tucson to oversee the affairs of the "Indians

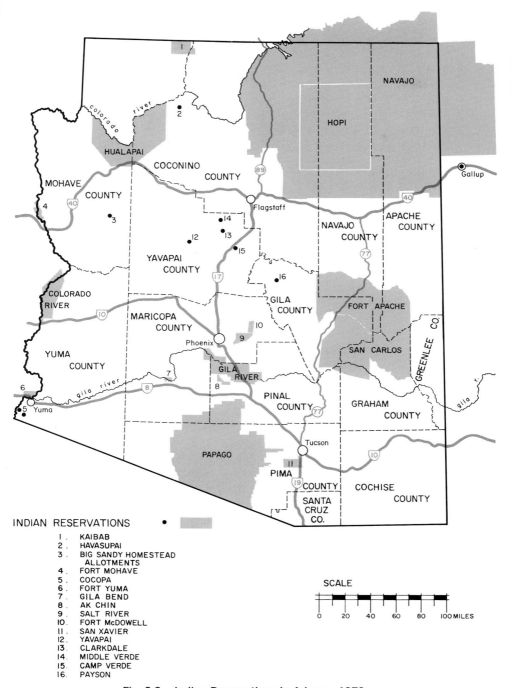

INDIAN RESERVATIONS   ●   ▨

1. KAIBAB
2. HAVASUPAI
3. BIG SANDY HOMESTEAD
    ALLOTMENTS
4. FORT MOHAVE
5. COCOPA
6. FORT YUMA
7. GILA BEND
8. AK CHIN
9. SALT RIVER
10. FORT McDOWELL
11. SAN XAVIER
12. YAVAPAI
13. CLARKDALE
14. MIDDLE VERDE
15. CAMP VERDE
16. PAYSON

SCALE

0   20   40   60   80   100 MILES

Fig. 3.3   Indian Reservations in Arizona, 1973.

included with the Gadsden Purchase." These were principally Papagos, Pimas, Maricopas, and a few peaceful Apaches living on the outskirts of Tucson. He arrived in 1857 and stayed until 1861 when the outbreak of the Civil War thoroughly disrupted the concern with Indian affairs in the New Mexico Territory. It was while Walker was still agent, however, that the first Indian reservation in Arizona was established. This was the Gila River Indian Reservation, set aside by an act of Congress dated February 28, 1859, for the Pima and Maricopa Indians living along the Gila River.

This reservation-making policy lasted in Arizona from 1859 to 1916 when the Papago Indian Reservation became one of the last such reserves in the United States. Only three small reservations, two for Yavapai Indians in Arizona (Prescott in 1935, and Clarkdale in 1969) and one for the Yavapai — Tonto Apache people (near Payson in 1972) have been established since then. Boundaries of other reservations have been altered appreciably, but with these exceptions, new ones have not been constituted.

There were three routes open to Indians to acquire land in Arizona during the mid-nineteenth century, all requiring some form of assent by the United States. These were by treaty, act of Congress, or executive order. Congress, either through direct legislation or through Senate affirmation of a treaty and the president of the United States, by issuing an executive order, could set aside public lands for exclusive Indian use and occupancy. Tribes "owned" their lands only through the largesse of the United States. Such ownership could be impaired either by revocation of an executive order or by subsequent acts of Congress — including unilateral revocation of treaties. In Arizona only the Navajo Indian Reservation was created by a Senate-ratified treaty in 1868. All other reservations still extant came about either by executive order or by an act of Congress.

By the Act of March 3, 1871, Congress brought an end to the negotiation with the Indian tribes by treaty: ". . . No Indian nation or tribe within the territory of the United States shall be acknowledged or recognized as an independent nation, tribe, or power with whom the United States may contract by treaty." The creation of reservations by executive order continued, however, until Congress acted in 1919 to prevent further additions to Indian lands by this means. Since then Indians have either purchased additional lands or have relied on Congressional action to expand their real estate holdings.

Assimilation in Isolation

It appeared to non-Indians involved in Indian affairs in the 1860s that there were only three alternatives to the solution of the "Indian problem": kill them; keep them on reservations in a perpetual state of dependency living a parasitic existence; or alter Indian political, social, and economic institutions to make them more like those of western civilization, institutions which had taken Europeans about thirty centuries to develop.

Between the 1850s and the 1870s, administrators tried to assimilate Indians by working within the old legislative framework. Teachers, farmers, blacksmiths, and carpenters, whose jobs were to educate natives, were assigned Indians and were housed on Indian reservations. These same men were often also responsible for the discipline of the Indians. It was during this period, moreover, that Indians became enclaved in large numbers. Reservations took on some of the aspects of open air jails or prisons without walls. Indians were expected to remain on the reservations and to behave properly — all the while learning about non-Indian society in total isolation except for contact with a few Indian service employees.

The Role of Churches

In 1865 the federal government began making contracts with various Protestant missionary societies for establishing Indian schools to teach agricultural and industrial arts. Missionary societies were paid $75 for each pupil enrolled in the program. Federal money continued to be spent to support church-operated Indian schools until 1900.

When U. S. Grant became president, he was persuaded by a group of Quakers that they should advise him in the appointment of Indian agents. This soon led to a policy in which various religious organizations, largely Protestant, submitted the names of nominees to the president for his decision. Thus the Reformed Church was assigned the task of offering lists of nominees as agents for the Colorado River, Pima and Maricopa, Camp Grant, Camp Verde, and White Mountain (Apache) agencies. Such special treatment was discontinued by Grant's successor, Rutherford B. Hayes, and by 1882, reservations were open to all religious denominations.

Schools

Late nineteenth and early twentieth-century attempts to force the assimilation of American Indians "into the mainstream of American life" were carried out with a vengeance through the schools. In 1887 the commissioner of Indian affairs ordered that all instruction in Indian schools be in English — and in many instances Indian children were punished for speaking their native language, even on playgrounds. In

1892 Congress authorized the commissioner to make school attendance compulsory; and in 1893 he was further authorized to withhold government rations from parents who refused to allow their children to attend schools. Many of the schools to which parents of small children objected most strenuously were off-reservation boarding schools. Large numbers of Indian children were forcibly removed from home to be sent to such schools, where the attempt was to make them think, act, look, and to be in every way possible like members of the dominant, non-Indian population.

If schools were seen as a principal means to force the assimilation of American Indian culture into that of non-Indian culture in the post-Grant period, so was Indian property. Carl Schurz, who was secretary of the interior under President Hayes, said as early as 1877 that "the enjoyment and pride of individual ownership of property is one of the most civilizing agencies." It should be remembered that private ownership of land was a concept altogether foreign to the American Indian. Land, like air, was something to be shared and used by everyone. Thus tribes and Indian communities owned the use rights to property, including reservation lands; no single person had title in fee and did not understand the concept.

Another extension of the arm of federal control became the matter of the issuance of rations. Indians defeated in war, like the Apaches and Navajos, became virtually dependent upon government rations of food, clothing, and tools in their new situations of confinement on reservations. This made the Indian agent, as the man in charge of issuing the rations, an even more powerful figure. It was during the period of the 1870s and 1880s — with large stores of food and other supplies going gratuitously to Indians who, confined to their reservations, would have perished without them — that dependency relationships were established between some Indian tribes and the federal government.

The final blow of this policy of forced assimilation seems to have come about in 1896. It was that year in which the order came from Washington that all male Indians be required to wear their hair short. If nothing else, it indicates that Indian male hair styles had been seven decades ahead of their time!

Criminal and Civil Jurisdiction

State and territorial laws and courts had no jurisdiction over Indians for crimes committed on reservations nor control over litigation involving whites and Indians regardless of where the offenses occurred. It was federal law alone which pertained to Indian reserves. The source of this peculiar legal situation, which remains current in Arizona, lay in the fact that as Britain, and later the United States, was expanding the western frontier, the central government found it necessary to reserve to itself the right to deal with Indians.

The Articles of Confederation, approved in 1781, contained a section heavily influenced by Benjamin Franklin which read:

The United States Assembled shall have the sole and exclusive right and power of . . . regulating the trade, and managing all affairs with the Indians, not members of any States, provided that the legislative right of any State within its own limits be not infringed or violated.

Thus the principle, however vaguely worded, was accepted that the federal government should manage Indian affairs and regulate Indian trade. At the same time, the notion of "Indian Country" became strengthened. "Indian Country" became all those areas outside state boundaries forbidden to settlers and unlicensed traders and subject to federal authority.

In September of 1783, just five months after the United States had made peace with the British, Congress issued a proclamation formally forbidding the settling on lands inhabited by Indians outside state jurisdiction and buying or otherwise receiving lands without Congressional approval.

The Constitution of the United States, which went into effect March 4, 1789, had less to say about Indian affairs than the Articles of Confederation, but principles had not changed. What the whole matter finally boiled down to was a clause in the Constitution which noted that the federal government had the power to ". . . regulate commerce with foreign Nations, and among the several States, and with the Indian Tribes, within the limits of any State not subject to the laws thereof." The entire basis for subsequent legislation and judicial litigation involving Indians is found in the president's power to negotiate treaties and Congress's right to ". . . make all laws which shall be necessary and proper for carrying into Execution the foregoing Powers."

The last three decades of the nineteenth century saw other actions taken to hasten the remaking of American Indians into non-Indian molds. Until 1883, tribal custom usually prevailed in relations among tribesmen. That is to say, Indians could neither sue nor be sued, and while they could be tried in federal courts for offenses involving white men, there were no tribunals to try them for offenses against other Indians. Although Congressional sanction of Indian police forces had been given in 1878, it was 1883 before the secretary of the interior authorized courts of Indian offenses. By 1904, the "offenses" over which these courts had been given jurisdiction by the secretary were participation in various native religious dances, plural marriages, practices of medicine men, destroying or stealing property, payment of money for cohabitation, misdemeanors, and crimes involving civil suits. The prohibition of native religious dances and polygamy, and the suppression of native medical practitioners were especially offensive to most Indians, and they reacted to this "religious crimes code" by cloaking these activities in secrecy. Polygamy, while by no means universal, was not a "crime" in the framework of most native cultures.

Indians living on reservations became answerable in federal courts after 1885 for crimes of murder, manslaughter, rape, assault with intent to kill, arson, burglary, and larceny. Since then assault with a dangerous weapon, incest, robbery, and embezzlement of tribal funds have been added to the list. Indians can also be tried in federal court for violating federal laws which apply to Indian and non-Indian alike, such as counterfeiting, smuggling, and crimes relating to the mails.

Otherwise, offenses by Indians against Indians on reservations or offenses on reservations by Indians which involve no victim remain to this day solely the problem of Indian courts. This is especially so in Arizona, which expressly disclaims legal jurisdiction on Indian reservations.

Such was the background of United States law respecting Indians when General Kearny arrived in Santa Fe. And in the seventh decade of the twentieth century, traders on Indian reservations in Arizona must still be federally-licensed; it is impossible for anyone to acquire or lease Indian-owned reservation lands without initial approval of the United States government; Arizona continues to have virtually no legal jurisdiction over Indians on reservations; and federal authority continues to be supreme where reservation Indian affairs are concerned.

The General Allotment Act

In 1887 a law was passed which was to have almost as much impact on Indian life in the United States, including that in Arizona, as any law passed before or since. This was the Act of February 8, 1887. It has been variously known as the General Allotment Act, the Individual Allotment Act, or the Dawes Act, named for its sponsor, Senator Henry L. Dawes. When this law was passed in 1887, American Indians were still in possession of about 139,000,000 acres of land. When allotting ceased under provisions of the Indian Reorganization Act in 1934, Indians were in possession of 48,000,000 acres. In other words, from 1887 to 1934, Indians were dispossessed of an additional 91,000,000 acres of land — this time thanks to a law that was meant by many of its proponents to bring about a satisfactory solution to the so-called "Indian problem."

Principally, the Dawes Act allowed for the individualization of ownership of land by Indians. At the discretion of the president of the United States, tribally-owned lands could be parcelled out to individual Indians, usually at the rate of 80 acres of farm land or 160 acres of grazing land to a family head. Single persons over eighteen or orphans under eighteen were given half this amount. The United States was to retain title to the allotted land for twenty-five years, or longer should the President deem it desirable. At the end of twenty-five years, the allottee was to be given a clear, fee simple title to his land; the land would go on the tax rolls; and the allotment could be kept, sold, leased, or disposed of as the Indian allottee chose. The 1887 law bestowed automatic American citizenship on any Indian receiving an allotment, but this was later amended so that allottees became citizens only when they were given title to their land in fee simple. The Dawes Act further bestowed citizenship on any Indian who voluntarily lived away from his tribe and who adopted "the habits of civilized life."

The lands on any given allotted reservation which remained after other land had been parcelled out were regarded as "surplus." The United States — through the Office of Indian Affairs — could sell the "surplus" land in behalf of the tribe. Money from these sales was deposited in the United States Treasury in behalf of the tribes, where it earned 3 percent interest per year, a secure if modest amount of income. Only the United States Congress, and not the Indians, had final say concerning how tribal money deposited in the Treasury could be spent. Congress usually appropriated funds in the Treasury belonging to tribes to be spent on Indian education and "civilization." It was through sale of these "surplus" lands that Indians lost most of the 91,000,000 acres in forty-seven years.

Even before the twenty-five-year trust period provided for in the General Allotment Act had passed, the law was amended to make it possible to give allottees clear title to their lands much sooner. It became possible to sell, lease, or condemn allotments by administrative procedure. What this meant in most instances was that an agent could declare an allottee "competent" at any time before the expiration of twenty-five years, and he could issue the allottee a patent to his lands. Much Indian land was taken by fraudulent means by Indian agents who collaborated with land buyers.

For nearly all allotments which were not alienated from Indians, the initial twenty-five-year trust period was extended by the president of the United States. The Indian Reorganization Act of 1934 extended them "until otherwise directed by Congress." Today there are still large acreages of allotted Indian land held in trust by the federal government. And because many generations have passed since allotting took place, with most original allottees now dead, heirs have accumulated in geometric progression such that it is not uncommon for as many as forty or fifty people to own undivided shares in a twenty-acre plot of ground. The Dawes Act provided that in the absence of a will — and most Indians do not write wills — the heirs should be determined by the heirship laws of the state or territory in which the land is located. Very few Indian allottees — especially in Arizona — have the vaguest idea what state laws are in this regard. Moreover, individual Indian tribes have traditional ways of reckoning descent and heirship, and these are frequently in conflict with state laws. Needless to say, there is a great deal of confusion over the matter of allotments, and with each passing day, the number of heirs grow and the individual's interest in land becomes more fractionated.

Fortunately for most Indians in Arizona, only the San Xavier, Salt River, Gila River, San Carlos, and Colorado River Reservations were allotted. There are more than 650,000 allotted acres of land on the Navajo Reservation, both in Arizona and New Mexico, but this remains a small percentage of the total reservation acreage. In fact, reservation lands in Arizona allotted under terms of the Dawes Act comprise less than 3 percent of the total of Indian-owned land, the other 97 percent being owned in trust by tribes in undivided shares.

As early as 1875 it became possible under certain circumstances for Indians to acquire land under terms of various homestead acts, and a few Arizona Indians continue to hold trust allotments which were made on the public domain. The 1,030 acres of Walapai-owned lands at Big Sandy in Arizona are made up of such allotments, as are all 480 acres of Quechan-owned land in Arizona.

Allotments as such today are a serious problem only on those reservations where allotted acreages comprise a large percentage of the total reservation land base. These are the San Xavier, Gila River, and Salt River reservations. What has happened through time is that non-resident heirs, not presently active members of reservation communities, outnumber resident owners of the land.

The effect of the Dawes Act on the Indians of Arizona was much greater than one would suppose judging solely on the basis of numbers of allotments. The fact is that the law was passed in 1887 over the strenuous objections of most Indians, or at least over the objections of Indians who knew anything about it. The law therefore became the first, concerning Indians, passed by Congress which altogether disregarded the principle of mutual agreement. Mutual agreement — regardless of however much coercion may have been applied to get it — had been the principle of treaty making. Furthermore, virtually all earlier Congressional legislation directed toward Indians before 1887 had considered tribal problems, as well as historical and cultural differences among the various tribes. The Dawes Act made no such allowances. It was blanket legislation designed to affect all Indian reservations uniformly; as hindsight now shows, it was blanket legislation at its worst.

The Dawes Act set a pattern for bypassing Indian tribal organizations. Federal agents could, and did, deal with individual Indian allottees after 1887. Tribes had no legal control over allotted lands, and it was only in those places where native notions of political control over the land remained strong that allottees did not consider land as their personal, private property. Tribal governments weakened, and in the wake of this weakening there came increasing federal supervision and control.

The Dawes Act placed the burden of assimilation on the individual; it disregarded tribes and tribal rights. Taken with the simultaneous emphasis on boarding school education, we find a period in which the United States made an all-out attempt forcefully to assimilate American Indians. In 1901 President Theodore Roosevelt described the Dawes Act as ". . . a mighty pulverizing engine to break up the tribal mass," whereby ". . . some 60,000 Indians have already become citizens of the United States."[1]

4. Twentieth Century Legislation

Bernard L. Fontana

Housekeeping Years

THE OPENING OF THE TWENTIETH CENTURY was inauspicious. It had become apparent to many non-Indians that allotment of lands was not the solution to Indians' problems; but allotting dutifully went on. More and more employees in the Indian Service came under the rules of the Civil Service Act passed in 1884. While graft may have lessened, complacency seems to have set in. More Indian schools, both boarding and day schools, were opening for business in established patterns. Between 1905 and 1910 more general Indian legislation was enacted by Congress than in any earlier five-year period, virtually all of it uninspired. The period has been characterized by a former commissioner of Indian affairs as one of "chilled trance."[1]

In 1902 the Supreme Court, in Lone Wolf v. Hitchcock, recognized the authority of Congress to abrogate treaties which had been negotiated with Indian tribes — and while this had no immediate effect on any Arizona Indians, it served again to let all Indians know where they stood *vis à vis* the United States.

Congress amended the Allotment Act, most of which seemed to have been designed to make it easier to separate the Indian from his land. In 1907 Congress appropriated the first money earmarked specifically to suppress liquor traffic on reservations, a bit like locking the barn door after the horses have dashed away in panic. The next year a law was passed which made it possible to extend loans to individual Indians. In 1909 Congress provided a law for the supervision of Indian forests, and the position of forester was thereby added to the roster of Indian Service employees found on reservations.

By 1912, the Indian Service was assisting reservation Indians in the areas of health, education, property management, water supply (including irrigation systems), building and physical plant maintenance, law enforcement (including suppression of liquor traffic), and transportation.

Between 1900 and 1919 more than twenty executive orders were issued concerning Indian land in Arizona, including the creation of reservations for the Papago (as distinct from San Xavier and Gila Bend), Ak Chin, Ft. McDowell, Cocopa, and Kaibab. Between 1900 and 1933 Congress acted on Indian lands in Arizona more than eight times, creating the Camp Verde Reservation in the process.

For all practical purposes, allotting came to an end in the 1920s — largely the result of several setbacks suffered by non-Indians who tried unsuccessfully to acquire Indian lands. A drive that began in 1917 to force the issuance of patents in fee to all allottees was effectively halted in 1922. Also in 1922 the Bursum Bill — proposing Congressional legislation which would have forced the Pueblo Indians to prove ownership of lands or relinquish title to squatters who had been living on some of the Indians' acreage — went down in defeat. The figure of Secretary of the Interior Albert Fall, who later went to prison in the wake of the Teapot Dome scandal, loomed in the background. Finally, the proposed Indian Omnibus Bill of 1923, which would have provided for the end to all special status for Indian property, failed to become law. These reversals seem to have taken the steam out of the allotting procedure.

In 1924 the most significant piece of Indian legislation of the early 1900s became law, conferring American citizenship on all native-born Indians who were not already citizens via allotment, military service, or other means. The bestowal of citizenship on Indians, however, did not change the situation with respect to federal control of individual or tribally-owned property on Indian reservations. Neither did it affect laws applying to Indians as individuals. Indians living on reservations in Arizona, even though they are American citizens, are still not subject to state laws while they are on reservations.

The administration of Indian affairs by the Department of the Interior had become big business by 1926. The Office of the Commissioner of Indian Affairs had within it an Office of Chief Clerk and separate divisions of inspection, administration, medicine, purchase, probate, finance, land, irrigation, and forestry. All of these had Washington offices; some, like the probate division, land division, irrigation division, medical division, and administrative division were represented in field districts and agencies. There were nine districts in all, number 7 (Arizona) and 8 (Colorado, New Mexico, and Utah) covering Arizona and New Mexico's twenty-two agencies. A typical agency, in addition to having its superintendent (formerly the Indian agent), had a plant foreman with his construction foreman, carpenters, engineer, blacksmiths, and laborers; a chief of police and policemen; a clerk in charge of office work and a staff of interpreters, stenographers, and other clerks; farmers; livestock specialists, millers; shoe and harness makers; a deputy supervisor of forests and such assistants as timber clerks, cruisers, and forest rangers; a supervisor in charge of irrigation work and his many helpers; allotting agents; and, if appropriate, a supervisor in charge of gas and oil development. Those agencies with schools had full complements of teachers, supervisory personnel, and maintenance people; and there was either a contract physician or an Indian hospital with a full staff of personnel from the directing physician to the common laborer. Many of the people filling these jobs — mostly unskilled and semi-skilled — were Indians.

Key people in the federal government, especially in the U.S. Senate, decided that the time had come, in 1926, for a sweeping reassessment of the Indian question and of seventy-seven years of administration of Indian affairs by the Department of the Interior. It seemed to many that federal policies were bankrupt if not corrupt; that Indian Service personnel were engaged mainly in housekeeping activities or worse; and that the "Indian problem" was still with us. Responding to pressure, in 1926 the secretary of the interior, Hubert Work, authorized an economic and social study of Indian conditions. The job was turned over to the Institute for Government Research, a privately-financed foundation, and Lewis Meriam and his associates were chosen for the task.

The result was the so-called Meriam Report, a document published by the Johns Hopkins Press in 1928 under the title, *The Problem of Indian Administration*. The Meriam Report examined and criticized previous Indian policies — the allotment system in particular — and it recommended several sweeping reforms. It suggested that,

. . . the fundamental requirement is that the task of the Indian Service be recognized as primarily educational in the broadest sense of the word, and that it be made an efficient educational agency, devoting its main energies to the social and economic advancement of the Indians, so that they may be absorbed into the prevailing civilization or be fitted to live in the presence of that civilization at least in accordance with a minimum standard of health and decency.[2]

No sooner had the Meriam Report appeared than the United States Senate, which had earlier threatened to do so, undertook its own survey of Indian conditions in the United States. It lasted from 1928 to 1933.

The "New Deal" for Indians

The Johnson-O'Malley Act

The Meriam Report and the Senate's survey of the condition of Indian affairs in the United States contributed significantly to a new climate in Washington. It became possible for President Franklin Roosevelt's "New Deal" to flourish in the Indian country. Congress passed the Johnson-O'Malley Act in April, 1934, the first of a series of laws to have far-reaching effects on American Indians. The Johnson-O'Malley Act enabled the secretary of the interior to make contracts with states, territories, or private institutions ". . . for the education, medical attention, agricultural assistance, and social welfare, including relief of distress of Indians through the qualified agencies of each State or Territory."[3] The most vigorous application of the Johnson-O'Malley Act was — as it is today — in Indian education. It is through Johnson-O'Malley that local public school districts are paid money to keep Indian children in school.

In 1937 the Arizona legislature authorized the state board of education to contract with the federal government for Johnson-O'Malley funds. The first contract for $33,000 was signed in 1939. This figure has risen annually since then until in 1969 the Arizona State Department of Public Instruction received $4,510,007.28 in Johnson-O'Malley money. This legislation has made it possible for Indian children to attend integrated public schools, either commuting from a nearby reservation or from a Bureau of Indian Affairs-operated Indian dormitory near a public school. The federal-trust status of Indian lands makes them exempt from state or other local taxes, including taxes for the support of schools. Johnson-O'Malley money has made it possible for public schools to accept Indian children when they might not otherwise have been able, and for public school districts to be formed on reservations.

The Indian Reorganization Act

The Act of June 18, 1934 (48 Stat. 984), the Indian Reorganization Act — also known as the Wheeler-Howard Act — set the tone for United States and Indian relationships for the next twelve or more years. This act ended the further allotting of Indian lands; it removed the threat of forced patents in fee, which would have required allottees to become land-owning property-taxpayers whether they were prepared or not; and it authorized federal appropriations to enable tribes to buy back lands they had lost or to purchase other lands to add to their depleted holdings. No sooner did the Indian Service use some of this Indian Reorganization Act (IRA) money to buy 27,246.69 acres of land for the Acoma Reservation in New Mexico than Congress attached a rider to the appropriation bill under IRA to make it impossible to use any such money thereafter for land purchases in Arizona and New Mexico.

Further provisions of the IRA made it the responsibility of the secretary of the interior to prevent the erosion, deforestation, and overgrazing of Indian lands; establish a revolving credit fund; facilitate the adoption of tribal constitutions and corporate business charters; set up an educational loan fund; and allow tribes to adopt constitutions to veto the disposition of tribal assets, to spend certain funds without secretarial review, to hire legal counsel, and to suggest operating budgets. In general, the Indian Reorganization Act re-emphasized cultural units rather than individual units, and tribes, rather than persons came back into focus as the potential vehicle for desirable change. In the due course of time all but the Navajo and Prescott Yavapai tribes in Arizona adopted tribal constitutions under terms of the IRA, although few have adopted corporate charters.

Other New Deal Legislation

Other federal legislation during President Roosevelt's administration created such agencies as the Sub-marginal Lands Board, the Federal Emergency Relief Administration, Resettlement Administration, Rehabilitation, and the Federal Surplus Relief Corporation. Funds from these sources, along with money provided by the Bankhead-Jones Act, made it possible for Pueblo Indians to acquire the use of more than 665,000 acres of land between 1934 and 1944, about half of what they owned in 1933. Other tribes, like the Papagos, were similarly enabled to add lands to their reservations.

The decade of the 1930s also saw a shift in educational goals for Indians from white-collar to agrarian; from grammar school to community school ideals, and from a ban on native religious and other cultural practices to their encouragement. There was also a new emphasis on technical and professional training.

There was also a concentrated effort to cause more Indians to go to work for wages. An Indian division of the Civilian Conservation Corps (CCC-ID) was devised for Indian reservations, and reservation economic pumps were primed with federal money for repairing roads, building trails, clearing land for farming or for better grazing, improving water supply facilities, and for a whole panoply of projects aimed toward the improvement of the economic base of reservations. Indeed, some of these federal programs on reservations during the years of the Great Depression offered enough job security and paid sufficient wages that many Indians who had made successful adjustments to off-reservation living were enticed to return.

John Collier, who as commissioner of Indian affairs was captain at the helm of the U.S.S. Indian New Deal, saw what he regarded as five major innovations during his first four years on the job, 1932–1936. These were the passage of the Indian Reorganization Act; the attack on problems of conservation; an overall endeavor to cause Indians to go to work;

the prevention of further land losses and the development of a credit system for Indians and Indian tribes; and a considerable improvement in Indian education, especially from the standpoint of its aims. Moreover, some boarding schools were closed; enrollment at others was reduced; and community day schools supplanted boarding schools in importance. It was also during these years that the Indian Arts and Crafts Board was begun under sponsorship of the Department of the Interior.

Collier called the Indian Reorganization Act — which was the real basis of the New Deal administration of Indian affairs — a fine example of ". . . the bi-lateral, mutually consenting, contractual nature" of the government and Indian relationship.[4] Certainly the IRA made choices of action available to Indians unknown since 1871.

It is difficult to measure the full impact of the Collier administration on Indian affairs, partly because even now all results are not in. Many provisions of the Indian Reorganization Act are still in effect, and many policies instituted by Collier continue to be felt.

However, the Indian New Deal was not without its weaknesses. One of the greatest of these, perhaps, was the nature of Indian "tribes" in 1934. Collier himself has said that ". . . at the very core of the Indian Reorganization Act . . . is the revival, and the new creation of, means through which the Government and the tribes reciprocally, mutually, and also experimentally, can develop the Federal-Indian relation, and the Indian relation to the rest of the commonwealth, on into the present and future."[5]

Such a reciprocal relationship depended upon there being two parties in the first place: the federal government and a tribe. The fact is that in 1934 "tribes" had in many instances deteriorated to a point where they no longer had effective leadership or leaders; they were divided into divisive factions; or they were non-existent. Too, there were few Indians capable of understanding the fairly complex nature of "tribal" constitutions and business charters being proposed. Certainly in Arizona, in every single instance of a "tribe's" adoption of a constitution under the IRA, principally non-Indians — either Bureau of Indian Affairs administrators, lawyers, or others — formulated the major outlines of these documents and persuaded for their adoption. Virtually all constitutions are modeled after the Constitution of the United States, with their ultimate roots in English common law rather than in the soil of Indian tradition. The area in which Indians were allowed to govern themselves along more traditional lines was that of crime and its punishment. Tribal constitutions, then, provided for executive and legislative branches of government much like that of the U.S.; they provided for an elective government like that of the U.S.; but they failed to provide for a judiciary branch and for guarantees of "due process of law" which American citizens enjoy under the Constitution of the United States.

Although the Hopi Indians officially adopted a tribal constitution, its adoption was not concurred in by all the traditional political-religious leaders of the various Hopi villages. Thus the Hopi Tribal Council became spokesman for only a part of the Hopi population, mainly the so-called "progressive" element. It is regarded with suspicion by many Hopis, who see the tribal council — which was superimposed on traditional Hopi governmental structure — as an arm of federal government meddling in Hopi internal affairs.

The Papago Indians, whose IRA constitution was approved in 1937, had traditionally recognized only village or regional political organization. Papagos and Pimas shared a common culture, but did not share a single leader or set of leaders and did not recognize an overall "Papago" identity. The "tribe" which adopted a constitution in 1937 was really a group of Indians, speaking dialects of a common language, who in 1916 had come to share a common Indian reservation. An overall chairman and political districts had been totally foreign to them.

The experience of the Apaches on the San Carlos Reservation was probably fairly typical of that experienced by Indians on most Arizona reservations. The chairman of the San Carlos Apache Tribal Council for many years during the 1950s, Clarence Wesley, explained what the adoption of an IRA constitution had meant on his reservation:

> At San Carlos during the days of Superintendent Kitch, the contents of IRA were fully explained. . . . Under the supervision of Mr. Kitch, who was himself a lawyer, and some reservation people, Indians and non-Indians got together and drafted a constitution. . . . After the constitution was ratified an election of councilmen was held. With the new changes taking place and the new tribal business committee, as they were called then, lacking knowledge in their new undertaking, the beginning of tribal government was not easy. In fact, Superintendent Kitch was still the boss.[6]

In short the New Deal for Indians was based upon what Collier called their "grouphood," upon what social scientists speak of as "Indian group life" and "native social controls and native values." It was upon these that changes and innovations were founded rather than upon individuals. But history had moved its finger over the native landscape. Indian groups, Indian social controls and Indian values in 1934 had become so widely corrupted or disorganized that in fact proponents of the Indian

Reorganization Act were confronted with creating groups where there were none in any meaningful sense, of encouraging a demoralized people to institute forms of social control forgotten by all but the oldest among them.

Again, it is Collier himself who has characterized well the state of Indian affairs on the eve of the New Deal:

. . . Government invaded, past any and all of the structures of Indian life, to the individual as a fiat-decreed social isolate. Government's Indian Service became structured into a monolithic and authoritarian structure and a monopolistic one. Not only Indian initiative, but participation and consent became ruled out. Intervention by any other branch of the United States Government except Congress and the Courts, became ruled out; the Indian Bureau existed as an aggressive monopolist. Indian Service in its turn became, inevitably, by intention a regimented operation through bureaucratized robots; but at the top, Indian affairs came to be looked upon as the prerogative of local members of Congress.[7]

The New Deal, recalling that Civil Service came into effect for Indian Service employees in the 1890s, inherited an army of people who had worked under the old system. At worst, some of these people were martinettes. In other instances, some were paternalistic, stifling father-figures who treated Indians as if they were children. Most were simply men trying to do a job. Only in rare instances, were there persons who worked diligently to instill in Indians a spirit of self-help and self-determination.

Federal Veto Power

Finally, with respect to Indian self-government, most constitutions had in them a clause that became familiar to Indian politicians: ". . . subject to the approval of the Secretary of the Interior." In other words, over most issues the federal government, through the secretary of the interior, maintained a veto power over which Indians had no direct control; one might argue that IRA constitutions gave Indians the illusion of self-government.

Indian Employment

Under Collier's regime the Indian Service ceased to be an employment agency solely for self-seeking whites. Indians were given preferential treatment, by law, in hiring by the Bureau of Indian Affairs, and even the usual Civil Service requirements were waived. Of course, whether it is desirable to have large numbers of Indians dependent for their livelihood on a federal agency whose sole existence in turn depends on Indians is a question not easy to answer.

Loan Fund

In terms of dollars and cents, the Indian loan fund established by the IRA was possibly one of the most successful of its provisions. From June 30, 1936, to June 30, 1952, loans totalled $30,911,060. By 1957, $22,797,722 had been repaid and only $91,268 had been charged off. Thus, losses due to charge-off came to only 0.33 percent, a record any private loan company would be glad to have. What these figures conceal, however, is that Indians spent much of this borrowed money on projects which failed, and which provided only relatively temporary economic relief for tribesmen.

The Future of Tribal Government

It is an axiom of life that short-term views carry with them the longest-term consequences. A corollary is that assessments of long-range programs based on short-term results are the least fair, if not the least reliable. Programs instituted on Indian reservations during the New Deal administration have been bloodied in Congress, but many of them remain unbowed. Already there are signs that "tribal" organizations which existed only on paper in the 1930s, and which were kept together by non-Indian interests, are emerging in the late 1960s as truly viable organizations which may in the 1970s be able to operate apart from non-Indian help or interference. If not by the 1970s, then surely in the 1980s we will see Indian reservation governments worthy of the name — and another one, two, or three decades are nothing measured beside the span of time Indians have had to contend with non-Indians.

World War II put an effective end to the Collier administration of Indian affairs. The Bureau of Indian Affairs' budget was slashed, and the whole program rapidly lost momentum. Collier had been wrestling with the problem of "old school" field employees on the one hand, and with an increasingly disenchanted Congress on the other. In March of 1944 Collier defended his policies before the Senate Committe on Indian Affairs. His defense provides a fair summary of the New Deal Program:

> We have tried to energize the individual Indian and the group, and to equip individual and group with knowledge and skills to enable them to go into the white world successfully if they want to hold their own and to make their way where they are if they want to. That is the meaning of the Indian Reorganization Act and of all other major things we have been working at. . . . In brief, we have quit thinking about assimilation and segregation as

opposite poles and as matters of "all or nothing." They are oversimplifications of thinking which do not connect themselves with dynamic realities. Indians are more themselves than they have been for a long time, and they certainly are more assimilated than they ever were.[8]

Termination

John Collier's successor as commissioner of Indian affairs, William Brophy, was ill for most of his appointment (1946–1948) and he took no effective action. His successor, John R. Nichols, made few changes if for no other reason than because he served for less than two years in 1948–1950.

Under Dillon S. Myer, however, another turn in official Indian policy occurred. Myer replaced most of the people remaining in upper administrative echelons from the Collier era. He came into Indian affairs as the former director of the War Relocation Authority — the group responsible for the management of Japanese relocation camps during World War II.

Myer made himself unpopular with many influential Indians and friends of Indians by his attempt to impose a series of restrictive regulations governing Indian choices of tribal attorneys. The Indian Reorganization Act had provided simply for secretarial approval of choice of counsel and fees. So strong were protests from the Indians and from such organizations as the American Bar Association that the regulations were never put into effect.

The new commissioner also reorganized the lines of authority within the Bureau of Indian Affairs in such a way that the area directors became the key men, and superintendents — the men actually stationed on Indian reservations — became " . . . the servants or errand boys of the area directors," with little control over funds or personnel. [9]

Under Myer there was renewed interest by the Bureau of Indian Affairs in off-reservation boarding schools, and the commissioner stated flatly that ". . . the off-reservation education of Navajos is directed toward the preparation of these children for permanent off-reservation employment." [10]

Most significant, it was during the administration of Dillon Myer that serious discussions began between the Bureau of Indian Affairs and Congress concerning the matter of termination or withdrawal. The terms "withdrawal" or "termination" refer specifically to bringing to an end the special relationship between the federal government and American Indians.

Discussions were carried forward even more vigorously by his successor, Glenn L. Emmons, a Gallup, New Mexico, banker, and the man appointed by President Eisenhower as the thirty-seventh commissioner of Indian affairs.

House Concurrent Resolution 108

In 1953, the Eighty-third Congress, in its first session, unanimously endorsed a statement on Indian policy, designated as House Concurrent Resolution 108. This resolution, the impact of which is still being felt, continues to bring considerable anxiety to the Indians of Arizona, virtually none of whom — considering reservation communities — want termination of reservation status or withdrawal of federal services. The entire resolution follows:

> Whereas it is the policy of the Congress, as rapidly as possible to make the Indians within the territorial limits of the United States subject to the same laws and entitled to the same privileges and responsibilities as are applicable to other citizens of the United States, and to grant them all of the rights and prerogatives pertaining to American citizenship; and
>
> Whereas the Indians within the territorial limits of the United States should assume full responsibilities as American citizens: Now therefore be it
>
> Resolved by the House of Representatives (the Senate concurring), That it is declared to be the sense of Congress that, at the earliest possible time, all of the Indian tribes and the individual members thereof located within the states of California, Florida, New York, and Texas, and all of the following-named Indian tribes and individual members thereof, should be freed from Federal supervisions and control and from the disabilities and limitations especially applicable to Indians: The Flathead Tribe of Montana, the Klamath Tribe of Oregon, the Menominee Tribe of Wisconsin, the Potawatomi Tribe of Kansas and Nebraska, and those members of the Chippewa Tribe who are on the Turtle Mountain Reservation, North Dakota. It is further declared to be the sense of Congress that, upon the release of such tribes and individual members thereof from such disabilities and limitations, all offices of the Bureau of Indian Affairs in the States of California, Florida, New York, and Texas, and all other offices of the Bureau of Indian Affairs whose primary purpose was to serve any Indian tribe or individual Indian freed from Federal supervision should be abolished. It is further declared to be the sense of Congress that the Secretary of the Interior should examine all existing legislation dealing with such Indians and treaties between the government of the United States and each such tribe, and report to Congress at the earliest practicable date, but not later than January 1, 1954, his recommendations for such legislation, as in his judgment, may be necessary to accomplish the purposes of this resolution.[11]

House Concurrent Resolution 108 soon resulted in the termination of the special federal relationship with the Klamath, Grande Ronde, and Siletz groups in Oregon; four bands of Utah Paiutes and the mixed blood Utes of Utah's Uintah and Ouray Reservation; the Modocs in California; the Menominee of Wisconsin; the Yakooskin Band of Snakes in Idaho;

and the Alabama and Coushatta of Texas. In the words of Senator Arthur V. Watkins of Utah — for many years the champion of Indian termination policies in Congress — "Approximately ten thousand Indians were thus set on the road to complete citizenship rights and responsibilities."[12]

Public Law 280

Also in 1953, as a further step in the direction of termination, Congress passed Public Law 280. This law enabled states having express disclaimers of jurisdiction over "Indian country" — reservations — to acquire criminal and civil jurisdiction by amending or repealing their disclaimer laws. So far Arizona with its large Indian population has not indicated a desire to assume criminal and civil jurisdiction on reservations except in the area of game laws. The assumption of such jurisdiction would eliminate most tribal ordinances; it would make state and county laws applicable on Indian reservations; it would abolish tribal courts in favor of the usual courts of law, ranging from courts presided over by justices of the peace to various local and state courts; and it would be incredibly expensive. Arizona's disclaimer law reads:

That the people inhabiting said state do agree and declare that they forever disclaim all right and title to . . . all lands lying within state boundaries owned or held by any Indian or Indian tribe the right or title to which shall have been acquired through or from the United States or any prior sovereignty and that until the title of such Indian or Indian tribes shall have been extinguished the same shall be and remain subject to the disposition and under the absolute jurisdiction and control of the Congress of the United States.[13]

Although Public Law 280 gave Arizona the right to repeal its disclaimer and to assume full civil and criminal jurisdiction on Indian lands, the Civil Rights Act of 1968 (Act of April 11, 1968; 82 Stat. 77) modified it to the extent that tribal consent must now be sought and obtained before the state can extend its jurisdiction. The Indians would certainly resist at this juncture in history; and the state has shown little interest in burdening itself with the staggering costs entailed in operating courts, police, jails, and related activities.

5. Contemporary Indians

Bernard L. Fontana

BEFORE DISCUSSING THE INDIANS of Arizona further we should give some thought to the question, "Who is an Indian?" The question has many answers. Each depends on the situation. There are legal, cultural, administrative, political, historical, biological, genealogical, and folk definitions of "Indian," no two of which are identical. Some definitions, in fact, have nothing in common.

It can be argued that American Indians are those people who are descendants of the aboriginal, pre-Columbian inhabitants of the New World. But who are these descendants? How much Indian "blood" must one have to qualify, and how can anyone be certain of one's genetic heritage in terms of degree? Some modern tribal constitutions require enrolled members of the tribe to be "of Indian blood" without specifying degree; others demand "at least one-quarter degree of Indian blood"; and still others, different degrees.

Is a person an Indian who has lost his native language and traditions and become assimilated completely into non-Indian society? Is a man an Indian whose biological claim to being an Indian is tenuous but who culturally identifies with some Indian group and shares their language and traditions by virtue of upbringing rather than by "blood"?

How many native traditions must survive to entitle one's group to the "Indian" label? Can people who no longer speak an Indian language still be Indians?

These questions and many more have vexed administrators concerned with such matters as inheritance of Indian property and distribution of tribal assets among tribal members. They are of concern to anthropologists who are trying to learn from Indians. And they often dismay Indians themselves, many of whom no longer know precisely who they are in a cultural sense. Indians are conscious of the many differences which separate them from non-Indians; they are usually aware of at least parts of their own histories and cultural heritage; and they are occasionally bothered by the fact that they now wear white man's clothes, eat his canned goods, drive his pickup trucks, and drink his liquor.

The ways in which the problem of Indian identity have been solved are purely pragmatic. Either the question is ignored or each case is judged individually. With few exceptions, insofar as administrators are involved, the question has not been difficult to answer in Arizona. Here, it is felt, are Indians who really are Indians, without question. The tendency has been to accept a person as an Indian if he chooses to be identified as Indian. One important exception, however, involves the right of unassimilated non-reservation Indians to receive BIA general assistance benefits. The matter is presently in litigation in a case involving a Papago Indian from Ajo, Arizona.

When it comes to the matter of "tribe," we find little agreement on definition. In the field of modern Indian affairs, however, a "tribe" generally refers to a group of people who speak a common language, share other cultural traits which give them a distinctive way of life, and live on reservations under a single tribal council or are officially enrolled members of a tribe. In this sense, a modern tribe is often also a distinctive political entity.

Languages

Those who have relied on the Saturday matinee or, more recently, on television as sources of information about American Indians are sometimes surprised to learn that all Indians do not speak the same language. They never did. The image of the wagon train coming West with a single interpreter who could talk "the Indian language" is a false one. If a modern guide wanted to talk to all the Indians in Arizona in some tongue other than English or Spanish, he would have to know at least nine languages — and he would still have trouble making himself understood by everyone. To do an efficient job, he would have to know seventeen languages.

Indian languages spoken in America, and even in the American Southwest, are often as separated in history and in mutual intelligibility as English is from Chinese. At the same time, some southwestern languages are distantly related historically, even though speakers of one may not be able to understand speakers of the other; and some languages are sufficiently related that conversations between speakers of them is not a problem.

The situation is somewhat like that in modern Europe. German and French, though not mutually intelligible, are related in that both are Indo-European languages. At some time in the past they diverged from a com-

Fig. 5.1 Scenes from the 36th
Annual Papago Rodeo and
Fair, Sells, Arizona, 1973. Ven-
tures into music featuring
electronic sound, as well as
tribal beauty contests, are
signs of cultural elements
being adopted from the sur-
rounding society. The junior
"bull-riding" is a popular event
in the all-Indian rodeos held
in various Arizona communities each year.

mon linguistic ancestor. Even more closely related and generally mutually intelligible are Norwegian, Danish, and Swedish, but Basque, spoken by people living between France and Spain, is related to no other language spoken today.

Many native idioms have become extinct in Arizona since Europeans first arrived in the Southwest in the sixteenth century. Such endemic dialects as Kaveltcadom, Soba, Sobaipuri, Jocome, and Suma have disappeared as modern languages. On the other hand, the names of many surviving dialects could be added to the list contained in the table which follows. There are, for example, at least eight modern dialects of Papago, with names such as *Kokololoti, Kohatk* and *Totokwan.* There are also regional variations in spoken Navajo, Apache, Yavapai, and Pima which could be included.

In the twentieth century, Arizona Indians who speak different languages communicate with one another either in English or in Spanish; many Arizona Indians are fluent in three languages: their own, Spanish, and English. Theirs is a far higher level of achievement in this regard than that of the state's non-Indian residents. In former times many Indians could speak the languages of their immediate neighbors. Table 5.1 outlines the linguistic situation with respect to Arizona's Indians.

Few outsiders recognize the extent to which native languages are spoken today. Recent valid statistics are not available on the subject, but many Indians in Arizona, especially Navajos and Papagos, speak almost no English. As recently as 1952 the Bureau of Indian Affairs estimated that 49 percent of Arizona's Indians did not speak or understand English, a figure which included about 44,000 Navajos. The proportion of non-English speakers among Indians in the state is certainly much lower than 49 percent in 1971, but precisely how much lower is unknown.[1]

The continued vitality of Indian languages is illustrated in the story told about a Pima girl who recently graduated from St. John's Indian High School, a parochial boarding school near Laveen, Arizona. Upon graduation she applied for a job with the Mountain States Telephone Company as a telephone operator. Asked on the application form to list foreign languages in which she might be proficient, she neatly lettered in the space: "English."

Reservations

There are twenty-three Indian reservations in Arizona, including the huge and sprawling Navajo Reservation which also lies partially within New Mexico and Utah. Parts of the Fort Mohave Reservation are in Arizona, Nevada, and California, with all of its Mohaves living in California in and near the town of Needles. The Colorado River Reservation is in Arizona and California, but its residents are in Arizona. On the other hand, although the Fort Yuma Reservation (Quechan) is in California,

TABLE 5.1

Linguistic Relationships of Indian Languages Spoken in Arizona

```
     I. Na-Dene (order)
        A. Denean (stock)
           1. Athabaskic (family)
              a. Western Apachish (genus)
                 (1) Navajo (language)
                 (2) San Carlos Apache
                 (3) Chiricahua-Mescalero Apache

    II. Karok-Yuman (Hokan)
        A. Yuman
           1. Yumic
              a. Upland Yumish (Pai)
                 (1) Havasupai
                 (2) Walapai
                 (3) Yavapai
              b. Up River Yumish
                 (1) Quechan (Yuma)
                 (2) Mohave
                 (3) Maricopa
                 (4) Halchidhoma
              c. Delta River Yumish
                 (1) Cocopa

   III. Aztec-Tanoan
        A. Kiotanoan
           1. Tanoic
                 (1) Tewa (Hano)
           2. Numic
                 (1) Southern Paiute
                 (2) Chemehuevi
           3. Hopic
                 (1) Hopi
           4. Sonoric
              a. Pimish
                 (1) Pima
                 (2) Papago
              b. Yaqui-Mayoish
                 (1) Yaqui
```

some of the Indians have valuable agricultural acreage in homestead allotment lands on the Arizona side of the Colorado River. Some Quechans, moreover, live in Yuma, Arizona.

Not counting private and taxable lands owned by individual Indians or by Indian corporations, Arizona's twenty-three reservations and Quechan-owned lands encompass approximately 19,665,000 acres. This means that 26 percent of Arizona's land base is Indian-owned.

The classification of the Indians of Arizona by BIA administrative units and reservations is depicted in Table 5.2.

Off-reservation Population

The "reservation" classification of Indians fails to account for the many Indians living off-reservation and for important Indian settlements not directly involved with the Bureau of Indian Affairs. The BIA's "official" population figure for Papago Indians, for example, is about eight thousand, when there are more than eleven thousand Papagos. The remainder live off-reservation in Tucson, Phoenix, Ajo, Marana, and Florence and in out-of-state urban centers such as Los Angeles and Cleveland. The BIA as a matter of policy enumerates only those Indians who in its judgment are somehow involved with federal trust land.

In August, 1964, Congress approved a bill which deeded 202 acres of federal land to the Pascua Yaqui Association, a non-profit, land-holding corporation organized under the laws of the State of Arizona in 1963. The Yaqui Indians in this association are those people and their descendants who first settled on the outskirts of Tucson in 1921 at a place which came to be known as Pascua Village. Today more than four hundred Yaquis live in old Pascua, but eventually many will be resettled on the association's 202 acres of New Pascua which lie southwest of Tucson.

Yaquis and Mexican Americans living in the community of Guadalupe, south of Phoenix, have incorporated as the Guadalupe Organization (GO); there is a community of Yaqui Indians in South Tucson called Barrio Libre, and another Yaqui settlement in the Phoenix area. The federal government does not exercise trusteeship over Yaqui lands, and the more than one thousand Yaquis who live in Arizona do not appear in BIA statistics.

Navajos, Apaches, Lagunas, Hopis, Walapais, and Cocopas — in addition to Papagos and Yaquis — are significantly represented in off-reservation settlements. One such former community is that of the Yavapai-Tonto Apaches which was on the Tonto National Forest on the outskirts of Payson. These people lived within the area before it became a

TABLE 5.2
Indian Population and Land in Arizona

Agency	Reservation	Indians	Population Estimate	Acreage
	Area Office — Phoenix			
Colorado River	Colorado River	Mohave, Chemehuevi, Hopi and Navajo	1,730	225,995[1]
	Fort Mohave	Mohave	—	23,669[1]
Ft. Yuma Subagency	East Cocopa West Cocopa	Cocopa	101	528
	Ft. Yuma	Quechan (Yuma)	30[1]	480[1]
Ft. Apache	Ft. Apache	Western Apache	6,230	1,664,872
Hopi	Hopi	Hopi, Hano, Navajo	6,144	2,472,254[2]
	Kaibab	Southern Paiute	138	120,413
Papago	Gila Bend	Papago	244	10,337
	Papago	Papago	4,688	2,773,357
	San Xavier	Papago	574	71,095
Pima	Gila River	Pima, Maricopa, and Papago	7,992	371,933
	Ak Chin (Maricopa)	Pima, Papago	248	21,840
Salt River	Ft. McDowell	Yavapai ("Mohave-Apache")	335	24,680
	Salt River	Pima, Halchidhoma	2,345	46,624
San Carlos	San Carlos	Western Apache	4,709	1,877,216
Truxton Canyon	Clarkdale Middle Verde Camp Verde	Yavapai-Apache Apache-Yavapai Apache-Yavapai	690	581
	Havasupai	Havasupai	370	3,058
	Hualapai	Walapai	1,033	993,172
	Prescott Yavapai	Yavapai Yavapai-Tonto	90	1,558
[not yet assigned]	[unnamed]	Apache	85	85
	Area Office — Navajo			
Chinle	Navajo	Navajo	71,400[1]	8,961,784[1]
Ft. Defiance	Navajo	Navajo		
Tuba City	Navajo	Navajo, Paiute		
		TOTAL	109,091	19,665,446

[1]Figures are for Arizona and on-reservation only.

[2]Includes 1,882,082 acres held in joint use with the Navajo Tribe.

Source: Information Profiles of Indian Reservations in Arizona, Nevada, Utah, Bureau of Indian Affairs, 1970, Phoenix.

Fig. 5.2   Arizona Governor Jack Williams, right, congratulates Alexander Lewis in January, 1972, on reelection as governor of The Gila River Indian Community.

national forest in 1905, and until Congress gave them an 85-acre reservation in 1972, they were regarded as "squatters" on a small part of their former aboriginal domain. In 1969 Senator Goldwater and Representative Steiger of Arizona introduced identical bills in Congress to secure Tonto Forest land in trust for them. Until Congress approved a bill in their behalf and President Nixon signed it into law, water and sewer lines and electricity could not be brought into the community and no new houses could be built. The U.S. Public Health Service, however, had provided the people with contract medical services.

Off-reservation dwellers who are not officially enrolled members of their tribal organizations, or those who are members of groups whose lands have never been held in trust by the United States, also are not enumerated as "Indians" on most censuses and therefore reduce the total "Indian" population figures given in most published sources. The 1970 United States decennial census enumerated all American Indians by tribe regardless of residence or official enrollment, resulting in an approximate population of twenty-five thousand off-reservation Indians living in Arizona. (See chapter 6, "The Urban Indian," for further discussion.)

A Modern Overview

The Bureau of Indian Affairs

The United States government exercises a trust responsibility over Indian lands, and the federal bureau responsible for the administration of this trust is the Bureau of Indian Affairs. To administer Indian affairs nationally, the BIA today is subdivided into twelve units called area offices. These area offices are given the name of the city in which they are located and each is responsible for the management of a number of Indian agencies. The agencies, in turn, usually serve one or more reservations. In Arizona specifically, the Phoenix Area Office administers Indian affairs in Nevada, portions of Oregon and Idaho, Utah, and all of Arizona with the exception of the Navajo Reservation. The Navajo Reservation is so large that it has been placed under a separate area office at Window Rock serving the reservation in New Mexico and Utah.

A modern BIA agency is a rather complex organization. Although the tables of organization for agencies vary from reservation to reservation depending on local needs, a fairly typical agency is comprised of the superintendent (now the field administrator) and his office; a branch of administration, which includes supply and accounting; and branches or divisions of realty, housing, education, plant management, roads, land operation, credit, social services, reservation programs, employment assistance, and law and order. Late in 1970, for example, the Pima Agency had more than 115 Civil Service and wage-rated positions.

Tribal Bureaucracy

Set off against the BIA structure are the tribes' own bureaucracies. It is not surprising that the largest tribe in the United States in population as well as that owning the largest reservation in the country also possesses the most complex tribal bureaucracy. The Navajo Tribe even owns and operates its own tribal utility authority, and its police department is larger than sheriffs' offices in most Arizona counties.

Fig. 5.3 With wages earned on and off the reservations, Arizona Indians participate in a cash economy which brings them to commercial centers such as the Hubbell Trading Post in Ganado, Arizona.

A more typical tribal organization is exemplified by the Gila River Pima-Maricopa Community. In addition to a governor and lieutenant governor, there are a business manager, administrative assistant, comptroller, committees secretary, census clerk, receptionist, bookkeeper, secretary, treasurer, tribal judges, police chief, and seventeen councilmen. There are tribal committees, boards, or commissions for arts and crafts, education, farming, government and management, homesite, housing, irrigation, land, model cities program, planning and zoning, police, skill center, social development, and the youth home.

Modern Economy

Although some Indians continue to hunt, gather and farm, it would be erroneous to characterize the modern economies in this way. All of

Arizona's Indians are dependent today on cash economy; the earned incomes of Indians, as with non-Indians, are derived through the sale of labor and skills. Only a relatively few Indians earn money through the sale of farm products, and only the Navajos are largely dependent on sheep and other livestock, although cattle are important on the Papago, San Carlos, Fort Apache, and Walapai reservations. The cash income from the industry is divided among a small proportion of the total population of these last named reservations.

While outwardly most Hopi communities resemble Hopi settlements of fifty or even a hundred years ago, some have begun a kind of suburban sprawl. Non-contiguous houses are common today, and many Hopis live on isolated ranches. Moreover, the advent of electricity, television, piped water, and housing improvements may one day make it impossible to distinguish a Hopi village from an FHA housing project.

Widely scattered hogans, the forked-stick and six-sided houses that are almost symbolic of Navajo Indians, are now supplemented by urban developments at Window Rock, Fort Defiance, and Tuba City. This does not include the thousands of Indians who have forsaken their reservation homes — if not their languages and other aspects of their cultures — to live and to work in cities.

Dispelling Popular Beliefs

There are many traditional beliefs about Indians which persist today in spite of facts to the contrary. To dispel a few of these: in 1953 Congress amended Indian liquor prohibition laws, the first of which dated back to 1802, to provide for local option. Tribes can permit intoxicating beverages on reservations and control its sale as they choose. Fort Apache and Gila River are the only Arizona reservations which permit liquor. State liquor licenses are required, and hours and taxes are regulated by state law. Off-reservation Indians have only to obey state and local laws with respect to liquor as with all citizens.

Personal Taxes

Indians, like other citizens, are subject to federal income and Social Security taxes regardless of place of residence; Indians are subject to draft laws; Indians do not receive gratuities of money or goods merely because they are Indians. Indians pay no property taxes if their property is held in federal trust (as reservation lands are), but if they own land in fee simple or improvements off-reservation, they pay taxes just as others do.

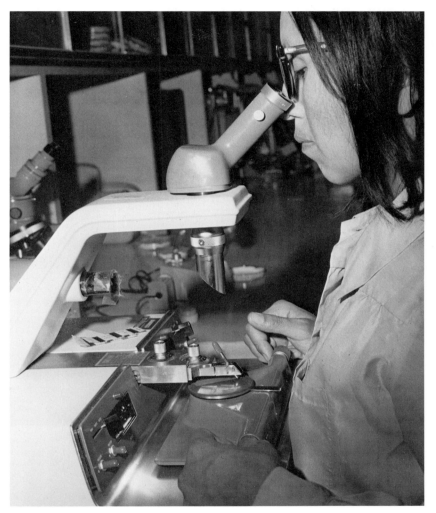
Fig. 5.4 Various federal programs help to train people in acquiring new skills and to place them in jobs on or near the reservations. This young woman is working at Fairchild Electronics in Shiprock on the Navajo Reservation.

Voting

Arizona and New Mexico were the last two states in the United States not allowing Indians to vote in non-Indian elections. Their laws were amended in 1948, and today, provided they meet the requirements set by law for all citizens, Indians can vote in federal, state, county, and city elections. Arizona required that its voters be literate in English, but the U.S. Supreme Court struck down this requirement late in 1970.

Land Claims

In 1946, Congress approved the Indian Claims Commission Act, enabling all tribes to sue the federal government before a special federal commission for certain causes. The five categories under which suits could be filed were: (1) claims arising under the Constitution, laws, treaties or executive orders of the president; (2) claims arising out of a civil wrong, such as a breach of contract, with respect to which the claimant would be able to sue in a regular court if the United States were to allow it; (3) claims based on treaties, contracts, and agreements made on the ground of fraud, duress, unconscionable consideration, or mutual or unilateral mistake; (4) claims arising from the taking by the United States of Indian lands without proper payment being made; and (5) claims based on fair and honorable dealings that are not recognized by any existing rule of law or equity.[2]

Before the Indian Claims Commission Act became law, it was necessary for tribes wishing to sue the federal government to get a special enabling jurisdictional act from Congress to present in the United States Court of Claims. Between 1881 and 1950, 150 such claims were filed, of which 34 were won by the Indians. Some of these cases, like that of the Winnebagos, continued from 1928 to 1942 before it was finally dismissed in favor of the United States.

In Arizona virtually all tribes have taken advantage of the Claims Commission Act to file suits before the Indian Claims Commission, nearly all based on the wrongful taking of land. The Quechans, Walapais, Havasupais, Southern Paiutes, and Yavapais have so far won claims and been compensated by the Claims Commission and Congress. The Pimas and Papagos have also won claims, but have not yet been compensated.

Employment Assistance

Although the Bureau of Indian Affairs has tried to find jobs for Indians off-reservations for more than sixty years, it was only under Dillon Myer that "Relocation Program" was instituted. Indians wishing to go elsewhere to work or for job training can get financial assistance from the bureau. About a million dollars was appropriated for this purpose in

1956, a figure which rose to three-and-a-half million in 1957. Indians still receive BIA assistance to relocate to urban centers in Dallas, Los Angeles, Cleveland, Chicago, and the San Francisco Bay Area for training in secretarial skills, welding, tool-and-die making, and dozens of other occupations. The difficulty is that once trained, many Indians return to the reservation, where few opportunities exist for the application of their newly-learned skills.

Industrial Development

In the last decade, the bureau has placed ever-increasing importance on the relocation of industries to reservations. Under the rubric of "industrial development," the idea is to take advantage of reservation resources — natural, human, and man-made in the form of tax advantages and federal financial backing — to give Indians greater options. Those who wish to stay on reservations to work may, if the program succeeds, be able to do so; those who wish to leave the reservation can be helped to do so under older programs.

Federal Services to Indians

Most recently, legislation has extended many other federal programs previously available only to non-Indians. Assistance to Indians is available through the Department of the Interior and the Bureau of Indian Affairs in the form of Adult Vocational Training; American Indian Credit and Financing; American Indian Industrial Development Program; Relocation Program; Reservation Adult Education Program for American Indians; and Social Services to American Indian Children.

The Department of Agriculture can provide Farmers' Home Administration Financial Assistance to Small Towns and Rural Groups; Farmers' Home Administration Loans to Cooperatives; Farmers' Home Administration — Emergency Loans Administering Agency; Cooperative Extension Service; Farmers' Home Administration, Rural Housing Loans.

Through the United States Department of Labor, Indians are offered Experimental and Demonstration Projects for Rural Persons; Real Property for Residential, Commercial, Agricultural, Industrial or Public Uses or Development; Neighborhood Youth Corps; Experimental and Demonstration Projects for the Mentally Retarded; Experimental and Demonstration Projects under MDFA; Experimental and Demonstration Projects for Youths and Adults with Limited Ability to Read and to Write; and Youth Opportunity Centers.

Since 1955 the Department of Health, Education, and Welfare has been responsible for the health care of Indians, having assumed the administration of hospitals and clinics from the Bureau of Indian Affairs. The

United States Public Health Service, Division of Indian Health, now supplies all reservation and Indian hospital medical personnel and free medical care. Health, Education, and Welfare also offers the following: Sanitation Facilities and Service for American Indians; Community Health Planning; Community Health Services for Chronically Ill and Aged; Cooperative Research Program; Child Welfare, Research, and Training Demonstration Projects; Child Welfare Services; Demonstration Projects in Public Assistance; Federal Credit Unions — Loans and Thrift and Financial Counseling; Guidance, Counseling, and Testing; Identification of Able Students; Old Age Assistance; Services for Older Americans; Vocational Rehabilitation; Adult Basic Education; Correctional Rehabilitation Study Program; Juvenile Delinquency and Youth Offenses Prevention and Control; Student Assistance for College Work; and the Work Experience Program.

The Department of Commerce, chiefly through its Economic Development Administration, offers technical assistance grants for the development of reservation industrial parks. The Department of Commerce can also provide other public works and economic development programs.

The Office of Economic Opportunity funds reservation Community Action Programs, including legal services and community development programs; Volunteers in Service to America (VISTA workers), many of whom are on reservations; and reservation-located job corps training centers for young men and women, many of whom are American Indians.

The Veterans Administration and the Small Business Administration are also involved on today's Indian reservations, and with American Indians generally.

The overwhelming trend in the past few years has been toward the diffusion of responsibility for the administration of Indian affairs. The United States Public Health Service already runs a close second to the Bureau of Indian Affairs in manpower and monetary expenditures on Indian reservations. The popularity among Indians of essentially Indian-run Community Action Programs under the Office of Economic Opportunity has forced BIA administrators to improve their programs. The bureau finds itself increasingly in a coordinating role, but even so, as trustee of Indian-owned lands, it continues to exercise economic control — whether implicit or explicit — over the lives of reservation Indians.

Nixon Policies

The policy of the Nixon administration with respect to Indian affairs is one aimed at lessening federal control and creating greater participation of Indians in decisions which affect their future. The Bureau of Indian

Affairs is hoping to contract many of its present services to tribes or private organizations. The trend is toward an increasing number of public or other types of non-BIA schools controlled by Indian boards. Reservation "superintendents" are now called "field administrators," and much of the authority of the area directors has now been given to the field administrators. Preference is being given to industrial lessors of Indian lands who will include Indians in managerial and administrative positions.

Although it may be possible within a relatively few years for the BIA to divest itself of direct involvement in law and order, education, plant management, roads, land operations, housing, credit, employment assistance, and various reservation programs and social services, as long as the United States holds Indian lands in trust a BIA will continue to exist.

A cynic might argue that there is something contradictory in the sponsorship by the federal government of a "program" of Indian "self-determination." It is almost as if we are telling Indians when and how they shall determine matters for themselves.

Arizona's Involvement

The interest of Arizona's legislators in Indian affairs has been largely constrained by the jurisdiction of the federal government. However, in 1954 the Arizona Commission of Indian Affairs was created to "consider and study conditions among the Indians residing within the state" and to "accumulate, compile and assemble information on any phase of Indian affairs." It was intended to provide the state's Indians a more direct means of communication with the state. Its members, two non-Indians and five Indians, are appointed by the governor. The governor, superintendent of public instruction, director of public health and attorney general are ex-officio members. Since its inception the commission has held public meetings, conducted hearings, and published innumerable reports, guides, and directories.

When termination loomed on the horizon, the Bureau of Ethnic Research was established in 1952 at the University of Arizona, to research the social and economic problems of Indians in the event the State would have to assume responsibility for services previously provided by the federal government. During its twenty years the bureau has researched Indian problems in education, manpower, economic development, law, political and business organization, adaptation, administration, culture, health, population and demography, and land use.

Since 1959 Arizona State University at Tempe has had a special program in Indian education. The Indian Community Action Project

(ICAP) was established under the College of Education at A.S.U. in 1965, funded by the Office of Economic Opportunity. This contract expired May 31, 1970.

In the recognition of the need for the University of Arizona to become more deeply involved with Indian problems, the university president appointed a campus-wide Indian Advisory Committee. In 1968 the office of coordinator of Indian programs was established to further these efforts. The University of Arizona Agricultural Extension Service is now responsible for programs on all Indian reservations, and in 1971 the university established an Indian studies program leading to an undergraduate minor in the subject.

Northern Arizona University at Flagstaff has recently instituted a teacher corps training program, one designed expressly with Indians in mind. It has also established an Indian Manpower Technical Assistance Center.

Taxes

One of the major concerns of Arizona's leaders is taxes. Problems involving a state income tax for Indians earning money on reservations; taxing improvements built on Indian-owned industrial parks; taxing mineral products removed from Indian reservations through leasehold taxes — all are questions before the courts which are presently unresolved. Some Arizona legislators, keeping an eye on the copper boom on the Papago Reservation, have called for a leasehold tax. Others have suggested requesting various "in lieu" taxes from the federal government to offset loss of tax revenue occasioned by industries locating on reservation lands.

It has been pointed out, however, that reservation development brings increased buying power to Indians, and that reservation prosperity can help off-reservation prosperity as well. Coolidge, Casa Grande, and Chandler, for example, have enthusiastically supported current developments on the nearby Gila River Indian Reservation. The flow of cash onto reservations inevitably finds its way off the reservation. Like everything else where Indians are concerned, the issue is not clearcut. To term the inability of counties to tax copper mined on the Papago Reservation a "disaster" is probably to overstate the case. To the extent that tribes benefit from the counties' and state's losses may well be the extent to which this money finds its way back into the mainstream. All this may be fulfilling the moral obligation incurred by dispossessing Indians of their lands and many of their native rights in the first place.

There is nothing simple about solving the many problems which confront Arizona Indians today. Even agreeing on what the "problems" are is no easy matter. One thing is clear, however. Indians cannot help themselves or be helped by pockets full of platitudes, by gratuitous hand-outs of old clothes, or by maintenance of the wall of social and cultural isolation which has far too long sealed off any possibility of mutual under-standing. More than one hundred twenty years of Anglo domination of the Indians of Arizona have left both sides with a heritage of separatism that ill-becomes all of us and the future of our state.

6. The Urban Indian: Man of Two Worlds

Thomas Weaver and Ruth Hughes Gartell

ONE OF THE MOST NEGLECTED and least visible populations in Arizona is the urban Indian. He has most of the problems of Indians residing on reservations but unlike them he does not have the facilities or agencies available to meet his needs. Urban-based public agencies feel that the Indian is the responsibility of various federal agencies who help him on the reservation. The Indian in the city is often reluctant to push as hard as other minorities to get the services in welfare, education, health, and in other areas to which he is legally entitled as a citizen. The problem is not only attributable to the biases and misconceptions of public agency officials and to the inability of the Indian to take advantage of and press his demands for his share of these services, but because of his small numbers he lacks the visibility and organization to make his demands felt.

The present brief overview will direct itself to answering some of the following questions: How many urban Indians are there in the state of Arizona? Who are they? Where are they? Why do they come to the city? What problems do they have?

Population

Several problems are encountered in making statements regarding the numbers of Indians in urban areas. One has to do with the nature of the sources of data and the second with the nature of the population itself. It is well known that the U.S. Census report undercounts American Indians because of the many problems in deciding who is an Indian and because of the difficulties in conducting the census survey itself. Identifying an Indian did not present a problem in census surveys of areas completely encompassed by reservations. However, in rural areas, towns, and urban areas which were at some distance from reservations, Indians may have been classified in erroneous categories because identification of the Indian was left to the subjective judgment of the census taker. The enumerator completing the form during the household interview either asked the race question, judged by appearances, or relied on local knowledge of the ethnic identity of the family. This presents a special problem in the Southwest in that many Indians have Spanish surnames and thus are often counted as part of that population; also Indians are not always distinct physically from the neighboring population.

Another problem relates specifically to the nature of the urban Indian population. Many Indians reside in the city only while seeking or holding temporary employment. This often entails much moving from place to place in the city and between city and reservation. Thus, some Indians are part of that large number of transients in the city who may be referred to as "floating migrants," a population which is very difficult to pinpoint during the crucial period of census enumeration. Even given its inaccuracies, however, the U.S. Census report is the best available source for population statistics.[1]

The total Arizona population increased 36.1 percent from 1,302,161 in 1960 to 1,772,482 in 1970. This represented a 37.2 percent increase for whites, 22.9 percent for Negroes and 14.9 percent increase for Indians. The Indian population increased from 83,387 in the 1960 U.S. Census to 95,812 in the 1970 Census, but the proportion of American Indian to total population in the state has been declining through the years primarily because of the large in-migration of non-Indians. In 1890 the Indian population in Arizona represented 34 percent of the total population, compared to 5.4 percent in 1970.

The urban and rural distribution of population for Indians represented an almost perfect mirror image of the same distribution of non-Indians. Of the 1,772,482 persons in the 1970 population for Arizona, 80 percent were urban and 20 percent were rural residents. On the other hand, the total Indian population of 95,812 included 19 percent living in urban areas and 81 percent in rural areas.

Although the percentage of Indian population found in urban areas is small compared to the total state population, it represents a considerable increase over the last several decades. The 1950 U.S. Census enumerated 62,849 Indians of whom 2,995 or 4.5 percent lived in urban places. In 1960 Arizona's Indian population increased to 83,387 with 8,300 or 10 percent living in cities and towns. This compares to the 1970 population of 95,812 Indians with 18,174 or 19 percent in urban areas. Thus, the rate of urbanization of Arizona's Indian population is doubling every ten years. Based on an estimated state Indian population of 105,000 in 1980, if the same trend continues one may expect to find 35 to 40 percent or between 36,000 and 42,000 of the Indian population living in Arizona's cities and towns by 1980.

Fig. 6.1   The pull of tradition continues to attract urban Indians back to the reservation for such religious activities as this Apache puberty ceremony performed by Ga'an dancers near Beaver Springs, Arizona.

Although the Indian population increased in the state by 14.9 percent between 1960 and 1970, the increase varied in each of the state's fourteen counties. Two counties, Greenlee and Yavapai, decreased 34.66 percent and 12.05 percent, respectively. The remaining twelve counties showed an increase in Indian population ranging from 2.81 percent in Coconino and 5.17 percent in Apache counties to six counties with sizeable increases of 20 percent or better (Cochise, 40.74 percent; Gila, 30.68

percent; Graham, 34.66 percent; Maricopa, 37.15 percent; Pima, 20.9 percent; Santa Cruz, 29.41 percent; and Yuma, 26.08 percent). Coconino and Apache counties, with the lower percentage increases in Indian population, probably reflect natural population increase directly related to fertility and out-migration rates, but the counties with the largest percentage increase may reflect the national trend across the country of greater migration by Indians to the urban areas. The counties with the largest increases in Indian population also reflected the largest influx of total migrants, namely Cochise, Maricopa, and Pima counties.

The ten urban places in the state which contain 10,000 persons or more in the 1970 U.S. Census are Douglas, Flagstaff, Glendale, Mesa, Phoenix, Prescott, Scottsdale, Tempe, Tucson, and Yuma. They are located in Cochise, Coconino, Maricopa, Pima, Yavapai, and Yuma counties, which together account for 65 percent of the total population of the state of Arizona, 34.3 percent of the total Indian population, and 61 percent of the Indian urban population. The remaining 39 percent of urban Indians live in towns and cities having populations under 10,000 scattered throughout the state. This, of course, does not include the large percentage of Indians found in reservation urban places such as Bylas and San Carlos with populations of 1,125 and 2,542, respectively.

The increasing popularity of city and town residence for Indians is indicated by the listing in the 1970 U.S. Census of eighty-three places with Indian population totaling 19,796 persons. An indication of the growth of Indian population in the ten most populous cities in Arizona is provided by comparing the 1960 and 1970 U.S. Census surveys. These ten cities grew from 803,427 to 1,154,922 during that decade for a percentage increase of 43.75 percent. During the same period the Indian population in these ten cities increased from 4,843 to 10,540 for a percentage increase of 117.63 percent. Although the total number of Indians in each of these ten large cities is small, it is significant to note the following changes in numbers and percentages: Scottsdale, 19 Indians in 1960 to 249 Indians in 1970 for a 1,210 percent increase; Tempe, 53 Indians to 304 Indians for a 473 percent increase; Phoenix, 2,538 Indians to 5,893 Indians for a 132 percent increase; Flagstaff, 655 Indians to 1,324 Indians for a 102 percent increase; Tucson, 1,217 Indians to 1,926 for a 58 percent increase.

The following urban places also reflected increases in Indian populations in 1970. The percentage of the total population represented by Indians will provide an additional idea of the general distribution of the urban Indian population in the state: Ajo, 11.15 percent; Clarkdale, 10.2 percent; Coolidge, 4 percent; Flagstaff, 5.6 percent; Fredonia, 24.5 percent; Gila Bend, 5.7 percent; Grand Canyon, 17.2 percent; Holbrook, 11.2 percent; Page, 10.2 percent; Parker, 6.2 percent; Show Low, 6.4 percent; Snowflake, 6.7 percent; South Tucson, 9.6 percent; Thatcher, 4.5 percent; and Winslow, 13.8 percent.

Types of Urban Communities

One of the best ways to visualize Indians in urban communities is to discuss them in light of the following typology: reservation communities, reservation border towns, urban centers, and urban reservations. The Indians living in these urban places change with regard to the following characteristics: (1) total Indian population, (2) Indian percentage of the total population, (3) length of residence, (4) psychological attachment to or remoteness from the reservation culture, (5) socio-economic status, (6) level of acculturation, and (7) tribal composition. The reservation community, the border town, and the urban center can be placed on a continuum with regard to migration. In this way we can refer to a

Fig. 6.2   Indians who work in cities near the reservations frequently return for social and ceremonial participation. Oriole singers from Sacaton Flats sing traditional Piman songs while using a cardboard box for a drum, during the Mul-Chu-Tha, an annual fair held to raise money for youth activities in Sacaton.

"step migration" in which Indians move first to agency towns or reservation communities and from there to border towns and eventually to the larger urban area over a number of years or several generations. This model helps to explain the differences between urban Indian populations in the various cities and towns in Arizona.

The reservation community or agency town, as defined by Spicer and Nagata,[2] is generally found on the reservation around the sites of the BIA and tribal governments or around boarding schools, mission stations, and trading posts. Generally these are communities of a thousand or more which are primarily Indian, but which have various other non-Indians in small numbers, usually professional staff who work and live there. Generally, the Indians who reside and work there are from the reservation itself or nearby reservations. Examples of such communities are Tuba City, Window Rock, Fort Defiance, San Carlos, Bylas, Sacaton, and Sells. Bylas and San Carlos, for example are 97.2 percent and 91.2 percent Indian. The Indian living in such communities is usually very closely tied to the reservation culture and participates actively in its ceremonial and social life.

The second type of community, the reservation border town, is a city or town found near the reservation boundary. It has small shopping centers, or small businesses, which have been servicing a primarily rural and ranching culture for many years. The Indian constitutes a smaller percentage of the total population of the border town than of the reservation community. The Indian population is most likely made up of Indians from nearby reservations, but may also have Indians from other state reservations. Frequent participation in the social and ceremonial life of the nearby reservations is possible. They move on and off the reservation for short periods of time to take advantage of the financial, economic, and improved educational and other services available in these towns. Examples of reservation border towns and the percentage of the total population which is Indian are: Winslow, 14 percent; Holbrook, 11.2 percent; Snowflake, 6.7 percent; Show Low, 6.4 percent; Thatcher, 4.5 percent; Ajo, 9 percent; Gila Bend, 5.7 percent; Coolidge, 4 percent; Parker, 6.2 percent; Clarkdale, 10.2 percent; Grand Canyon, 17.2 percent; Page, 10.2 percent; and South Tucson, 9.2 percent. The last named city, however, creates a dilemma in terms of our typology. Because of its contiguity to Tucson proper it may well be considered part of the Tucson urban area. At the same time because of its contiguity to the San Xavier and Papago reservations it could be considered a reservation border town.

The characteristics of Indians who live in the major cities or urban centers differ significantly from those of the populations discussed so far.

The percentage of the total population which is Indian is much smaller than in other types of urban communities although the total number of Indians is larger. The Indian population in these larger urban centers is not made up solely of local Indians, but includes Indians from throughout Arizona and outside the state. They are less likely to take part in the reservation ceremonial and social life because of the greater distance of the urban center from the home reservation community. They are more likely to hold better jobs, stay longer in the city, and to have adjusted better to urban life. Examples of urban centers are the three largest cities in Arizona, Flagstaff with a population of 1,324 Indians, or 5.7 percent of a total population of 26,117; Phoenix with 5,893 Indians or 1 percent of a total population of 581,562. Tucson, if we include South Tucson as part of the metropolitan area, has a total of 2,523 Indians or 1 percent of a total population of 269,153.

The diverse tribal composition of the larger urban areas in the state provides a potential for pan-Indianism. Pan-Indianism, that is, the coming together of Indians from different tribes in common association for mutual help or social and recreational functions, has not been as fully developed in Arizona urban centers as it has in other urban areas in the United States. Kelly and Cramer reported in 1960 that tribes represented in Flagstaff included about 50 percent Navajo, 30 percent Hopi, and 20 percent other tribes, including representatives of the Sioux, Apache, Tlingit, Paiute, Tewa, Hualapai, and Eskimo.[3] The Phoenix population, in contrast, includes large numbers of Navajo and Apache Indians, with significant numbers of Papago, Pima, Hopi, and others. The nascent development of pan-Indianism is demonstrated by the presence of the Central Plains Indian Club, with members of the Sac and Fox of Iowa; the Omaha of Nebraska; the Cheyenne-Arapaho, Choctaw, Comanche, Osage, Pawnee, Shawnee, and Ponca, all of Oklahoma; Flathead of Montana; Sioux of South Dakota; and Winnebago of Wisconsin. The Tucson Indian Center, on the other hand, is made up mostly of Papago and Pima, with some representatives from other Arizona tribes such as Apache, Navajo, Hopi, and such out-of-state tribes as Cree, Sioux, Seri, and Choctaw.

Indians living in larger urban centers are more likely found in some sectors of the city than others, and with the increasing influx of Indians to the city over the past twenty years, these sectors are growing rapidly. Flagstaff's Indian population grew from 275 in 1950 to 655 in 1960, and to 1,324 in 1970. This population centers on the east and west sides of town near the railroad tracks and in the southern part of town along U.S. highways 66 and 89. The bulk of Indian population in Phoenix is found in the southwest quarter, south of Camelback Road and west of 16th

Street and in Tucson in a south central sector bounded by Silverbell, Speedway, Campbell, and south 12th streets. In 1950 the U.S. Census reported 789 Indians in Phoenix, increasing to 2,538 in 1960 and 5,893 in 1970. Tucson had 150 Indians in 1950, 1,217 in 1960, and 1,926 in 1970.

A fourth type of urban settlement may be distinguished as an urban reservation, that is, an enclave of Indians belonging to a single tribe or from a single reservation who live in an enclaved community within a larger town or city and who associate with each other more than with Indians from other tribes. Examples of the urban reservation include the Laguna Colony, which has been in Winslow for many years; Barrio Libre, a community of Yaqui Indians in South Tucson; Guadalupe, south of Phoenix, where Yaqui and Mexican Americans have incorporated as the Guadalupe Organization; and another Yaqui community in the Phoenix area. The Pascua Yaqui Association, a non-profit, land-holding corporation organized under the laws of the State of Arizona in 1963, was deeded 202 acres southwest of Tucson in August, 1964, by a Congressional bill. This area, known as New Pascua, is inhabited by Yaquis — and their descendants — who first settled on the outskirts of Tucson in 1921 at a place which became known as Pascua Village. In the early seventies, there were still more than four hundred Yaquis living in this older community, but eventually many will be resettled in New Pascua. The federal government does not exercise trusteeship over Yaqui lands, and the more than one thousand Yaquis who live in Arizona do not appear in BIA statistics.

Although the 1970 U.S. Census counts less than 20,000 Indians living in urban areas, the fact that Indians are part of a floating migrant population, together with knowledge that Indians move off the reservation for short periods of time to accomplish short-range goals such as earning enough money to buy a car, or refrigerator, or other such commodity, it can be safely stated that there are probably well over 20,000 Indians living in urban environments in the state. One could easily hazard a guess of an urban population of from 25,000 to 30,000 particularly during the time of the year when there is a high labor demand in the cities, such as during the winter tourist season.

Motivations for Moving

The motivations compelling some Indians to leave the reservation are complex and varied; yet it is apparent that many Indians come to the city for reasons that are overwhelmingly economic. In most studies of

Fig. 6.3   The old and the new styles of dress intermingle freely in the 1970s.

this subject the motivation most frequently cited is that of finding a job.[4] Unemployment is high on most reservations, and the Indian with a strong motivation to better his economic condition must seek employment off the reservation, either on a temporary or permanent basis. The strength of this motivation, and the degree of economic success subsequently achieved are important indicators of whether or not the Indian will stay in the city.

Strong as the desire for economic betterment may be, other less readily apparent motivations are perhaps as effective in influencing the Indian to try life off the reservation. Arizona tribes as a whole are distinct from many other Indian groups in the U.S. in that for the most part they have retained their native language and an aboriginal land and cultural base.

But it is hard to maintain cultural integrity against the pressures of poverty, governmental policies, and against the frustrations of the young who want the best of both worlds.

Thus many younger Indians leave the reservation in search of the adventure and increased opportunity that city life seems to offer; and also for easement of their responsibilities to tradition and for a more general identity with other Indians instead of just their own tribe. Yet there is much in city-life that seems hostile and uninviting.

For many young Indians, the pan-Indian movement offers a solution to this conflict. By offering the individual Indian an identification with "Indianness," a particular perspective that many Indians — despite their tribal origin — can share, pan-Indianism enables the individual to maintain his Indian identity, while escaping both what he may perceive as the unfriendliness of the white world, and at the same time, certain restrictions of a specific tribal identity. When such an organization exists in a city, it can help ease the adjustment by offering companionship, aid, and a sense of purpose. However, for many Indians, tribal rivalries persist in the city, and such pan-Indian feelings and cooperation are not possible.

But both the old and the young, those seeking economic advancement for themselves and their family, and those seeking adventure and increased opportunities, need the support and security of home ties. Thus, the Indian is faced with conflicting pressures which pull him toward the city, and at the same time press him to stay at home with family and kin — with those who "speak his language" and share his way of life. As Nagata succinctly puts it:

> The Indian is confronted with the alternatives of staying on the reservations, which are economically underdeveloped and yet secure in . . . tradition, or of migrating to cities which provide possible access to material comforts and freedom from conservative restraints, yet also can cause personal disorganization and a feeling of uprootedness among . . . strangers.[5]

For many Indians in Arizona this conflict is somewhat alleviated by avoiding the move to major cities and seeking employment in smaller cities closer to home. There is much evidence to suggest that Indians more easily establish residence in cities with the following characteristics: (1) medium size, (2) tolerant social climate, (3) proximity to home reservation, (4) employment opportunities in governmental agencies, (5) culture contact of long duration.[6] But even in this compromise situation, which would apparently enable the Indian to retain his traditions while bettering his economic condition, there remain strong pressures preventing a successful or easy accommodation to the demands for participation in two cultures that this compromise entails. Many of these pressures are specifically related to the Indian's lack of preparation for the complexities of modern American society; equally a problem is a lack of understanding or concern for Indians on the part of the larger society. The locus of both these problems is in the cities, where the confrontation or differences in values and life styles is met head on.

Another arena of more subtle conflict in early 1973 is the reservation. The greatest hope of many Indians today is to keep and develop reservation lands economically so that life on the reservation will be self-sustaining and the young people will not have to leave. Recently, federal, state, and tribal agencies have begun to promote this policy, and funding has been made available to promote economic development. Still many Indians live with the fear of termination and the ultimate loss of their lands; they fear that if too many leave the reservation, federal support for reservation programs will be withdrawn and shifted to aid urban Indians. They fear that if the young and newly-educated leave, taking talent and training with them, any hope of developing the reservation will be gone as well. Thus, leaving the reservation with intentions of permanently settling in a city may be seen as a kind of betrayal.

At the present time there seems to be some direct competition between the urban and reservation Indian for federal funding. At a meeting of the National Indian Manpower Task Force in June, 1971, tribal leaders would not agree to the sharing of allotted funds with urban Indians. A separate fund had to be set up for urban Indians.

On some Indian reservations in Arizona sanctions remain rather strong to prevent their members from being drawn into white society. The Papago, for example, discourage intermarriage by ruling that such a couple must live off the reservation. The use of Emergency Employment Act funds on this reservation is another example of this attitude; no funds are used for training that would lead to off-reservation jobs.

At the same time, though urban Indians in fact

> . . . have the same property rights in regard to tribal holdings as those who live on the reservation . . . the management of these property rights is being handled by those Indians who live on the reservation and have a voice in tribal government. The off-reservation Indian has little or no voice in the disposition of his own property.[7]

From time to time a group of off-reservation Indians may band together to alleviate this situation, but without success. A group of Papagos living in Tucson and Ajo were recently denied non-voting representation on the Tribal Council.

Most Indians, thus, have a good deal to lose if they commit themselves to leaving the reservation on a permanent basis. This partially

Fig. 6.4 Majestic natural surroundings of the reservation often are sufficient pressure to keep the Indian at home or to cause him to want to return. Looking north from East Rim Gorge into Supai country.

explains why the population of Indians in urban areas is so mobile. A relatively small group is in fact committed to staying; most are in the city on a temporary basis out of dire economic need, and while in the city make every effort to return to the reservation as often as possible to maintain kinship ties and obligations, and to remain eligible for important ceremonial roles. This is the group of Indians least prepared for city life; ironically they often lack the training and skills necessary to secure the badly needed job, or the experience and confidence to cope with supermarkets, super highways, housing problems, used car dealers, loan companies, banks, bills, doctors, and dentists and all of those other "minor irritations" that can make life so frustrating even for the experienced. For this group there is at least the refuge of return to the reservation.

Those Indians who leave the reservation with an intention of permanently settling and succeeding in the city have certain advantages; usually they avail themselves of training programs sponsored by the BIA and other agencies, and even receive help, advice, and financial aid while in the process of resettling. Yet this is the Indian who is the "invisible man" — as the reservation shuts its gates behind him, he and his problems remain generally unrecognized by the white man. He is the man of two worlds, yet unseen and ignored by both.

Problems of the Indian in the City

Only recently have efforts been made to create job opportunities for the Indian on the reservation. Tribal councils, in cooperation with federal, state, and privately funded agencies such as the BIA, the Economic Development Administration (EDA), Small Business Administration, the Arizona Civil Rights Commission, the National Alliance of Businessmen, the Indian Development District of Arizona (IDDA), the Four Corners Regional Commission, and the Arizona State Department of Economic Planning and Development have made great strides in bringing industry and business to the reservations and greatly increasing the job opportunities for Indians on or near the reservation. Many Indians feel that, at last, efforts to aid the Indian are being aimed in the right direction: developing the reservation itself, rather than training the Indian for jobs in the city.

Nevertheless, for the foreseeable future, large numbers of Indians will continue to come to the cities. There are a number of reasons for this: one is that the Indian population is increasing. In 1960 the Navajos, for example, were the most rapidly growing segment of the U. S. population. This trend, although less marked in the seventies, continues. More people require more jobs, and the present rate of economic development of the reservations simply is not sufficient to keep up with the growing demand for jobs.

The Indian is a much neglected member of the urban population, and his numbers are growing and his problems increasing. Finding employment is his major problem, but poor educational background and training is a basic cause of his difficulties, and must be considered a major problem in itself. Finding and maintaining adequate housing, transportation, and obtaining dependable medical service are major obstacles to the Indian who first comes to the city. Discrimination exists; there are no statistics on it, but it is not the sort of problem that can be dealt with by citing statistics. The following piece was written by a Papago Indian in a local newspaper:

I am a Papago Indian very proud to be one, and what I want to say I hope you'll understand for I don't know much about the so-called English grammar.

The main problem I'm concerned with is unemployment for Papago Indians. Some of the problems I have in keeping a job I will discuss. I have worked with white people, but couldn't get along with them or maybe they didn't get along with me.

The people I worked with were all non-Indians. They talked behind my back (luckily I had a nosey friend to tell me all this).

They criticized the way I dressed. A great many Papagos disapprove of the white shirt and necktie bit. This is one reason why the Papago turns away clerical jobs, or vice versa. The Papago tries to be neat in every way — if he can afford it.

They criticized how quiet I was. They wished they hired someone else who'd be a little bit more lively. Well, this Indian isn't concerned about how much he should open his mouth, but rather how he should get his work done.

They criticized how rude I was not to say: good morning, good afternoon, hi, goodbye, etc., to every one of them. To the Papago it is silly to greet each other with the same word day after day after day, because it will only become meaningless.

The Papago, when greeting on a morning or anytime, will say what he wants to, but it is no greeting like "good morning." At times he will ask "Are you feeling fine," which I think has a little more meaning than the word, "Hi."

They criticized how rude it was not to introduce myself to a new person on the job. If a Papago wants to know who somebody is, he will ask someone else or he'll hear his name mentioned. You know, to the Papago it's quite funny to see people shake hands when introduced. Shaking hands is done only for religious purposes. When meeting a new person a smile shows the person is already accepted as a friend.

They criticized how rude I was not to say thank you when done a favor. To the Papago there is no such word. When a favor is done or a gift is given, he shows appreciation by returning something of equal value to the giver. (Those people never saw the favors I returned which meant thank you).

These are some of the reasons I was told to quit my job. So now I'm looking for another, knowing I'll face the same problems in the white society.[8]

In the alien and often unfriendly environment of the city, there is little he can take for granted, except perhaps the friendship of those Indians who have come before him.

Employment

Specific information on Indian unemployment is available for only a few reservations, and none is available for urban Indians as a group. Nationwide statistics on Indians provide a notion of the enormity of the problem:

Such figures as are available from the BIA and elsewhere, have indicated a range of unemployment from 12% to 74%, with an average around 40% (1969). During the winter season in some areas of the U.S., the unemployment rate reached 90%.[9]

Part of the reason for these extremely high unemployment statistics may simply be, according to the Arizona State Employment Service, that a rather large proportion of Indians are not in the labor force. Statistics for 1969 show a labor force participation rate of only 40 percent for five sample reservations, compared to 60 percent for the nation as a whole. Many Indians, helped by family ties and responsibilities, prefer to stay on the reservation, rather than leave to find work; many simply lack the training and education required to acquire a job. Thus the lower participation rate of Indians in the labor force only adds greater weight to the story told by the unemployment statistics.

The statistics available for Arizona Indians are perhaps slightly less alarming, but still indicative of a serious employment situation. The unemployment rate on the Fort Apache reservation is 7.3 percent (roughly twice the state and national rate), with the rate of labor force participation at only 44.5 percent, compared to 60 percent for the nation as a whole. Labor force participation rates are even lower on the San Carlos Apache and Papago reservations with respective rates of 41.2 percent and 30.9 percent. However, the San Carlos Apache have a relatively low employment rate at 5.8 percent compared to the Papago figure of 11 percent.[10] From these statistics it is readily apparent ". . . that Indian unemployment is far higher, and the median income lower, than that of any other significant ethnic group in the state."[11]

Figures available from a sample household survey in Tucson by the Department of Community Development (1969), although of a relatively small scale, certainly suggest that the economic and employment situation of Indians on reservations carries through to a large degree for Indians in urban areas. The sample of this survey was taken from neighborhoods in Tucson in which substandard housing conditions predominated. A total of 935 households containing 3572 persons were interviewed, with 4 percent of this population Indian; 60 percent Mexican American, 24 percent white and 11 percent black. Of this population, the unemployment rate of 40 percent for Indians was the highest, compared to 30.5 percent for blacks, 20.8 percent for Mexican Americans, and 13.3 percent for whites. Most of the Indian households (55.2 percent) had incomes of less than $3000 annually; at the same time 36.9 percent of these households contained six or more persons. The housing problem of Indians is very much a function of low income combined with large, often extended, families.

There are a number of organizations that recognize and attempt to alleviate the unemployment problem of the Indian. The primary aim of most of these agencies is to provide training and job placement, but some also help with related problems such as transportation and housing, which beleaguer the Indian when he first comes to the city, and often prove a significant handicap in his attempt to find employment. Low-cost, adequate housing is difficult to find; and discrimination on the part of some landlords often exaggerates this problem for the Indian.

Transportation poses an equally serious problem. Once again, due to a lack of specific data on urban Indians, we must make certain assumptions from what we know of conditions on the reservation:

A lack of available family transportation was revealed in the study. Low family incomes contribute to continued poverty and low labor force participation by depriving Indians of automobiles and trucks. Even if these vehicles are owned, it is probable that they are not maintained mechanically. Thus, Indians may have difficulties commuting from one part of their reservation to another to seek employment. Also, they are restricted in ability to drive to nearby towns or distant metropolitan areas where work might be available. Over 60 percent of Fort Apache and Papago families are either without or have limited access to transportation. Just under 60 percent of San Carlos families are isolated from lack of transportation. Only about one-fourth of Acoma and Laguna families are restricted in their travel.[12]

Employment Organizations

The following are the major organizations that the Indian may turn to for help in finding employment:

Arizona State Employment Service

The Arizona State Employment Service provides the same services to the Indian as to the rest of the population; these primarily consist of testing, placement, vocational guidance, and manpower information. There are no special programs for the Indian except in one sense; there are branch offices located on six of the nineteen reservations in Arizona, and each of these is staffed by personnel who are members of the tribe they serve. The urban Indian may use the services of whichever office he chooses.

Due to insufficient educational and employment background, special effort is required to develop jobs for Indians. ASES attempts to do this through

personal employer visits and telephone contacts. All news media are utilized to express to employers and the public the employment needs of Indians and to communicate to the Indian worker the availability of job opportunities.[13]

During the year 1970, a total of 8,993 Indians applied for the first time for ASES services. This is the second largest number of new applicants since the early 1950s when ASES extended its services and assumed primary responsibility for Indian employment. Job placements were made for 19,595 Indians in 1970 with 7,369 (37 percent) of these in the agricultural sector. Although this is 643 more than in 1969, this figure actually represents a general decline of placements in agricultural work. The reasons, according to ASES, may be that

. . . improved worker retention practices have reduced turnover, and . . . housing for seasonal farm workers has had to meet more stringent standards . . . With better housing, Indians may tend to stay at a particular farm longer.[14]

There were 12,226 placements in non-agricultural jobs. Of these, placements in professional, sales, and clerical occupations total 571, a 32 percent increase over 1969; however the figure still represents somewhat less than 3 percent of total placements. Service jobs make up 30 percent of the placements and the remaining 30 percent are jobs of a trade and industrial nature. The Indian is still receiving the jobs at the bottom of the economic and social scale; although the statistics indicate that conditions may be improving somewhat.

Funding made available by the Manpower Development Training Act is the primary resource tapped by ASES for aiding Indian applicants. Through MDTA, needs are being identified, and programs developed to teach useful and competitive job skills, as well as to upgrade education and provide pre-vocational orientation. There are two basic kinds of MDTA projects — institutional and on-the-job training — to which ASES refers its Indian applicants. Other organizations to which ASES refers applicants are the Job Corps training centers and Neighborhood Youth Corps openings.

Arizona Commission of Indian Affairs

The Arizona Commission of Indian Affairs was established by the Arizona State Legislature in 1953 to study the conditions of Arizona Indians, and to provide an information base for the legislature and other agencies concerned with Arizona Indians. However, the commission has come to take a more active role, often acting as liaison between the reservation and the public. Once again urban Indians may be only indirectly affected, as the main focus of this organization is the reservation.

Employment Assistance Branch of the BIA

This is a BIA service that provides job training and placement of the reservation Indian. Often this necessitates relocation in the city, in which case the program provides assistance in finding housing, and enough money for basic subsistence — rent, food, clothing — until the first paycheck. A BIA official in the Employment Assistance Branch stressed that one of the most difficult problems of relocating in the city is finding housing, especially for large families.

There are fourteen employment assistance offices in the two Arizona agencies; these are divided up into what are called "origin" and "destination" offices. Origin offices are on or near reservations and help advise and relocate the Indian who is interested in employment of a permanent nature off the reservation. Destination agencies are in areas where Indians are employed and trained. In 1970, a total of 911 Indians took part in this program; 356 were from the Navajo area, 337 of whom were placed in jobs on the reservation. However, none of the placements from the Phoenix area were on a reservation: 432 were in the state, and 123 were out of state. It should be noted that this program does not aid the Indian who is already in the city; but only the Indian who originates from the reservation.

Indian Centers

The Indian centers in Tucson and Phoenix are among the few service organizations for Indians actually operated by Indians. The basic aim of these organizations is to help Indians with the immediate problems that face them in the city; high on the list of course is the problem of employment. Both of these organizations have small scale programs to help Indians find jobs. Due to a lack of funds these programs are of an informal and personal nature; the director keeps in constant contact with employment agencies, church organizations, and helpful individuals.

Much of the emphasis of the Tucson Indian Center is to create an atmosphere of community and friendship for Indians who have come to Tucson. The center is a place where Indians may come together for enjoyment, and to help each other. In this it is not completely successful, for while the center is much used by the Papago, it is rarely used by the Yaqui, the other major Indian group of this area. Although the Phoenix Indian Center is a comparatively smaller facility and less of a social center, it remains a place where Indians new to the area may come to make contact with other Indians.

Another common problem the centers try to alleviate is the lack of transportation; currently the Phoenix Indian Center is limited to two service vehicles; whereas the Tucson program consists of a car pool. Certainly both of these attempts prove to be only partial solutions. However, the vital need for this transportation service is shown by the fact 41.9 percent of those who use the Indian center in Tucson regularly avail themselves of this service.

Other services offered by one or both of the centers are food programs for children, alcoholism counseling, adult and consumer education, medical aid, and assistance in finding temporary and permanent housing. Certainly this list of preferred services is indicative of the very urgent needs of Indians in the city.

Health

Obtaining health services is a confusing and often difficult procedure for the urban Indian. He may continue to use the Public Health Service facilities which serve the reservation, or he may choose (or be required) to use county, private, or social service facilities.

The matter of the right of the urban Indian to continue to use the PHS service on the reservation is still unresolved. In strict terms the government is contracted to serve only those Indians on the reservation, but in actuality there is a wide variety in adherence to this policy. In a report on Indians in Phoenix, Judge Magnum reports that although "The off-reservation Indian is not eligible for these services . . . none who appears for emergency service is turned away."[15] The term "emergency" may of course be construed to include a wide variety of situations. The policy in Tucson is that urban Indians are accepted without question.

However PHS funds are not unlimited, and in the foreseeable future the PHS may have to discontinue its service to urban Indians in order to maintain adequate service to the reservations.

The use of county facilities by the urban Indian has also been a confused issue. As recently as 1971, Indians living in Tucson were not admitted at the county hospital unless they were on welfare. A number of Tucson Indians are still under the impression they must use the services of the PHS *only*. To compound the confusion, it was not until 1966 that the PHS Indian Health Clinic at San Xavier extended its service to include off-reservation Indians. Prior to this the only reliable medical service available to the Indian in Tucson, other than a few small, scattered and not widely publicized social service agencies, was the physician in private practice. This is, of course, the type of medical service used by most of the population; but for the Indian, accustomed to PHS, there are many difficulties involved in using this service.

Often the Indian simply cannot afford the service of the private physician; even if he does have enough money, he often lacks sufficient familiarity with medical "culture" to know how to find a good doctor, how to make and keep an appointment, and how to describe his symptoms. Generally, if the Indian can obtain service at the PHS, he prefers to do so; not simply for financial reasons, but also to be among people who understand his ways.

There are a number of services, like the PHS, that are in principle designed only for the reservation Indian. But a problem exists in determining at what point a reservation Indian becomes an urban Indian. The majority of Indians spend some part of their lives in the city. Many of these Indians return seasonally, others may stay in the city indefinitely, but still consider themselves "reservation" Indians. Currently the trend in the BIA is to consider an Indian "urban" after a year in the city. Should this criteria be enforced by the PHS, which it almost inevitably will, urban areas will have to become more involved in providing health care to Indians.

Besides the problems involved in obtaining health care, the urban Indian also shares in the health problems of the Indian population as a whole. Only general statistics are available, and once again, we can only surmise the degree to which the altered living conditions of the urban Indian may change the nature of his health problems.

The average age of death of American Indians is forty-four years; all other Americans average a life span more than twenty years longer (to age sixty-five). Concomitant with this, the average infant mortality rate of the Indian is twice the national average. Yet, alcoholism is conceived by many Indians as their number one problem. Alcoholism indeed may be the root cause of other Indian health problems, and problems of social adjustment as well. In turn, lack of employment, a problem that we have already discussed, may be a major factor precipitating alcoholism. One informant noted that many Indians come to the city looking for a job, meet with frustration and disappointment, and end up in the bars spending their remaining resources in an effort to forget. Alcoholism may be the source of other health problems, as it generally is combined with poor nutrition and vitamin deficiencies; in this run-down condition the Indian may be particularly susceptible to colds, infections, and contagious disease. Alcoholism also lends itself to increased accident proneness. Neglect, on the part of alcoholic parents, may also account for poor health conditions and increased accident rates of Indian children.

Alcoholism in the Indian family has far greater social repercussions than in the American family. Because his immediate kinship network is more extensive than the comparable American family unit, the alcoholic Indian parent or other family member affects more people.

The socially dysfunctional affects of alcoholism are well known, but for the Indian the effects are magnified. Drinking is illegal on most Indian reservations; thus most Indians have developed a pattern of drinking, not in the privacy and protection of their own home, but in bars, in the city, and under the scrutiny of the public eye. Often another (and more serious) aspect of the Indian drinking pattern is aggression. These two aspects of Indian drinking frequently bring the Indian into direct confrontation with the law; thus, the number of Indian arrests related to drunkenness has been used as one of the very few available indices of the extent and seriousness of the drinking problem. Barber, in his 1959 study of the Yaqui Indians of Arizona (a group that is completely urban) discusses the relationship between Indian drinking and arrests. He states that the fear of getting into trouble with legal authorities seems less important to the Indian than the need to become intoxicated or get into a brawl. He also states that while a few of the men may be mild alcoholics,

the drinking of the young men in most cases, though heavy is not compulsive. However this makes no difference as far as being arrested for drunkenness or attendant rowdiness goes, and probably half of the men have been taken in for this at least once.[16]

For much of the recent past the governments' attitude toward Indian alcoholism has been to prohibit the use and sale of alcohol on reservations. Alcohol control has been left to the individual reservations since 1948. Indians seem to feel that it is useless to attempt to solve the problem of alcoholism by itself, because it is the expression of other more basic problems, and that only when these are solved will alcoholism abate. Other Indians claim that Indian drinking is no greater problem than alcoholism in the larger society; but more publicized due to the fact that most Indians must still drink off the reservation in public places, and hence, are more visible than more frequent drinkers. Yet some small scale efforts have been made to deal with the problem. Alcoholism counseling is one of the services offered by the Indian centers. The Alcoholics Anonymous Program, however, does not seem to be a very successful approach to the problem of Indian drinking.

Although the significance of the statistics on Indian arrests for drunkenness is not clear, they are too large to be ignored. Statistics compiled in 1969 by the U.S. Senate Subcommittee on Indian Education are illuminating:

The vast majority of arrests, fines, and prison sentences in the Indian population are related to alcohol, and Indian arrest rates are also notoriously high. In one state penitentiary, Indians constitute 34% of the inmates whereas only 5% of the State's population is Indian. The majority of the crimes were committed while under the influence of alcohol.

In 1960, alcohol-related arrest rates of all Indians was 12.2 times that of the U.S. population generally. Drunkenness alone accounted for 71% of Indian arrests.[17]

Education

The Indian who comes to the city has generally already received his education. That this education has often been brief, has removed him from his family and culture, and almost always ill-prepared him to find employment is well known. These problems have been discussed elsewhere in this book. But the problems that face the children of the urban Indian seem somewhat different. Most of these children, unlike their parents, attend public schools; often they are in the minority, and generally there are no special education provisions for them. What are the effects of this new kind of educational environment upon the children of urban Indians?

First, it should be noted that perhaps "new" environment may not be so different from the old educational environment as appearances might indicate. The public system of education has, after all, been the model for the BIA educational program; one of the principal criticisms of BIA education has been that the BIA has duplicated the typical classroom found in any white middle-class neighborhood in the U.S. Special provisions for Indian students have been mostly temporary and subject to change. Even English has been taught, not as a second language, which it generally is for most Indian students, but by the same methods used to teach children who have known no other language than English. Perhaps one of the few real differences between the parents' and the child's school experience is that *in* the city the Indian child will most often be in the minority, and this difference may well prove to have a major effect. However, on the positive side, the traumas of being sent away to boarding school will not be duplicated in the urban Indian child's experience.

Something else to be noted in examining the difference between the urban and reservation education experience is the pattern of attitudes toward education. The Indian who has become fairly acculturated to the city (and this often involves being employed and having a relatively stable economic existence) may very likely have developed attitudes regarding education more like those of the general population; he recognizes the importance of education for getting ahead. However, the Indian who has not yet found his place in the city very likely retains attitudes about education formed on the reservation. Often this attitude is one of resentment or apathy. After the child has reached the age of twelve, many Indian parents feel the child is old enough to make his own decisions and set his own course, relatively free from interference. Thus, many Indian children, unlike most Anglo children, do not experience the constant pushing and encouragement from parents to achieve in school. Without doubt the parents' attitudes carry over to the child and have a direct bearing on the child's success in school.

We have few statistics that give any meaningful indication of the nature of the urban educational experience; but those that have been compiled are worth looking at. Kelly makes a distinction between non-Indian-oriented and Indian-oriented education and between public, private, and federal schools.[18] Of the total sample of 5850 Indian children, 2763 (almost half) were attending non-Indian-oriented public schools. Kelly's main finding was that Indian children usually enter school at least one year later than most children and continue to lag behind in later years. Of the student population aged sixteen to eighteen, 86 percent were at least one year behind. Many were held back for at least one year during the primary grades (1-3). Indian students in public schools (grades 1-2) were held back at a rate of 8.7 percent, compared to a rate for students in federal day schools of 12.9 percent. But it is worth noting that Indian students in federal high schools are rarely held back in grade, while Indians in public high schools are retained at about the same rate as non-Indians. Average daily attendance at Indian-oriented schools (94.9 percent) are somewhat better than at non-Indian-oriented public schools (90.9 percent).

Bass, in a 1968 study, provides some further insight into the urban educational experience for the Indian.[19] He attempted to distinguish the factors which influence the Indian in the decision to continue his education after high school. For these purposes he divides his sample of graduates of high schools from Arizona, Nevada, New Mexico, Oklahoma, southern Colorado, and southern Utah into continuers (185) and non-continuers (99). The sample in itself is unique, for many Indian students fail to complete high school; in Arizona the dropout rate is 35 percent. Bass found that students attending public high schools were more likely to continue education in some form (80 percent); the percentage of continuers from federal schools was only 64 percent; private schools did better with 76 percent. Public schools also had the largest percentage of graduates who completed programs after high school, 55 percent compared to 47 percent for private and federal schools. Rates of public school graduates who enter and complete college were far higher than for students with a federal school education; 33 percent of public school graduates entered college and 10 percent completed, while only 11 percent of federal school graduates entered with 1 percent completing. Private schools had the highest percentage of graduates to enter college (41 percent), but slightly fewer (9 percent) of its graduates completed than those from public schools.

Bass offers no reason why public schools seem to have consistently produced more students who continue training after high school. But perhaps some related data may illuminate this question. Indians coming from high schools where they are in the minority were more likely to continue (80 percent) than graduates from schools where Indians were in the majority (70 percent). They were also more than twice as likely to enter and complete college.

Perhaps the only conclusions that we can derive from these statistics is that Indians who attend public schools, especially schools where they are a minority, are much more likely to take on the values and attitudes towards education which characterize the wider culture, and are much more likely to be able to continue training if they choose. However, it appears that public schools may be more difficult for the Indian student than federal schools, a point which is supported by the lower attendance rates in public elementary schools and higher dropout rates in public high schools. In other words, if the student *survives* the educational experience provided by the public, non-Indian-oriented school, he may be better prepared and motivated to continue his education than his fellow Indians in federal schools.

Some of Bass's data, however, indicates that the Indian who con-

tinues his training may not be notably more successful than the Indian
who seeks employment immediately after high school; neither group was
particularly satisfied with present jobs:

> Interviewees were asked if they planned to change their general line of
> work within the next year. Responses indicated that many Indians, especially
> males, were unhappy with their employment. Less than 50% of the men indi-
> cated that they contemplated no change in the ensuing year. There were no
> appreciable differences in responses by continuers and non-continuers.[20]

Part of this may be due to the fact that often jobs must be accepted that
are unrelated to training.

> Twenty percent of the females and twenty-five percent of the males
> indicated that initial jobs were unrelated to their training. The most prevalent
> reason given for accepting an unrelated job was that work was needed and a
> job for which training had been received was not available.[21]

This is an all too common and discouraging problem for the Indian who
has made an attempt to better himself through vocational training or
higher education.

Why is "education" such a difficult and unsuccessful experience for
the Indian? Most of the reasons are readily apparent. For a long time
"education" has been an effort to turn the Indian into a white man, and
a lower class one at that. These efforts have been resisted. Now educational methods are changing, but attitudes are harder to change. Until
the Indian is completely confident that education is not a means of
depriving him of his culture, this attitude of resistance will linger.

There are some problems of a more practical nature that may be
dealt with over the short term. Failure to adequately learn to read and
write English has been a life long handicap to many Indians. More and
more it is being recognized that methods of teaching English to Indian
children must be specialized to accommodate the fact that they are
learning English as a *second* language.

7. The Legal Basis of Tribal Government

Emory Sekaquaptewa

THERE ARE SEVENTEEN INDIAN TRIBAL governing bodies operating within the geographic boundaries of the state of Arizona. Although they have lands in the state, the Quechan of the Fort Yuma Reservation and Mohave of Fort Mohave are situated in California. However, there are more than sixteen tribal groups or bands of Indians that comprise these governmental units, and it needs to be emphasized again that the term "tribe" has diverse meanings as indicated in chapter four. This diversity exists because of the uses of the term in the ethnological, political and legal sense, and in the sense in which the Indians themselves use it. Without adopting a specific definition of the term "tribe," the following discussion gives some historical legal information about tribal governments as distinct entities recognized by the Congress of the United States. These governing units are listed below with their corresponding tribal groups:

Governing Unit	Tribal Group
1. Ak Chin	Pima and Papago
2. Camp Verde	Yavapai-Apache
3. Cocopa	Cocopa
4. Colorado River	Mohave, Chemehuevi, Navajo, Hopi
5. Fort Apache	Western Apache
6. Fort McDowell	Yavapai
7. Gila River	Pima, Maricopa
8. Havasupai	Havasupai
9. Hualapai	Hualapai
10. Hopi	Hopi, Hano (Tewa)
11. Kaibab	Southern Paiute
12. Navajo	Navajo
13. Papago	Papago
14. Prescott	Yavapai
15. Salt River	Pima, Maricopa
16. San Carlos	Western Apache
17. To be named	Yavapai-Tonto Apache

Generally, the governments of the Arizona tribes are fashioned after a democratic form of government by popular rule through free elections. There are, of course, variations in social and political structure due to cultural differences. All of the tribal governments, except Navajo, are organized under a constitution adopted pursuant to the Congressional Act of June 18, 1934, commonly called the Indian Reorganization Act. However, the Prescott Yavapais have preferred to call their instrument "Articles of Association" rather than a constitution. These constitutional governments vest the powers in a tribal council chosen through free elections. These powers include those delegated by Congress, and powers inherent in aboriginal tribal sovereignty as recognized through Congressional statutes, Supreme Court decisions, and treaties.

The Navajo tribal government operates under regulations promulgated by the secretary of the interior on authority from the treaty with the Navajos and from statutes of Congress based on its sovereign and constitutional powers. The Navajo tribal ordinances and resolutions, permitted under the regulations of the secretary of the interior, have been codified into a form patterned after the Code of Federal Regulations. This codification is considered to be the "Constitution" of the Navajo Tribe. In practice, however, there is general similarity in all Arizona tribal operations in that all tribal councils are the central units of government exercising legislative control, at least in theory, over other branches of government and over the local units. Other branches usually include administration, judiciary, and local units such as districts, chapters, or villages, depending on the particular tribe.

Since not all tribal governments have assumed complete control over the administration of governmental functions necessary to serve the modern-day needs of the Indian community, some functions are provided by the Bureau of Indian Affairs under rules and regulations of the secretary of the interior published in Title 25 of the Code of Federal Regulations. It is dangerous to assume that these governments operate under some strict uniformity in terms of their powers, in terms of their amenability to some other governmental power, and in terms of their internal sophistication. Time and space will not permit discussion of every variation as to its legal and political significance; therefore, to state a general rule uniformly applicable to all tribes for their legal and political characterization becomes a very difficult task.

The realities are that these governments operate within the state of Arizona with varying degrees of independence from both federal and state governmental control; that there are Indian reservations variously created through treaty, statute, and executive order; and that the reserva-

Fig. 7.1   Indian self-government includes the election
of officers at a council meeting.

tions are occupied by Indians whose direct ancestors, for the most part, occupied the same areas long before the founding of the national republic. Their autonomous existence is legally recognizable through a long history of relations beginning with the American colonial governments, and later, with the federal government under the Constitution.

What is a tribal government, as a question to be more fully answered, must go beyond the mechanical structure of tribal governments and what they do. One authority states that Indian self-government includes the power of an Indian tribe to choose its own form of government, to define conditions of tribal membership, to regulate domestic relations of its members, to prescribe rules of inheritance, to levy taxes, to regulate property within the jurisdiction of the tribe, to control the conduct of its members by municipal legislation, and to administer justice. Viewed in these terms, the tribal government appears to be like a municipality, and it has been so characterized. It should be quickly pointed out that while ordinary municipalities look to either the federal or state authorities for their power and are creations of either of them, this is not so with tribal governments. Tribal governments are not creations under federal or state systems, but rather, are entities predating them by virtue of which they have retained residual powers not yet expressly extinguished by some act of the United States. In principle, this means that, "It is only by positive enactments, even in the case of conquered and subdued nations, that their laws are changed by the conqueror."[1]

The exercise of this tribal power is equally recognized whether it comes through customs handed down by word of mouth or through written constitutions and statutes, for the laws of the tribe owe their force to the will of the members of the tribe. Then, how do these tribal governments fit, if they do, into the more familiar institutions under the federal and state systems? A look at the historical origins of tribal governmental powers and how they have been recognized and reconciled to federal and state powers of government might help us to understand better the nature and place of tribal governments.

Since the federal government is founded on the Constitution and derives its powers from it, so the several states by consenting to join the Union through ratification of that Constitution have subjected their sovereignty to the superior power of the national government. But the Indian tribes are not states even though they are recognized as "distinct, independent, political communities, retaining their original natural rights,"[2] and, therefore, never had the opportunity to decide how they should fit into the national Constitutional scheme. While the Constitution, constructed as it was in contemplation of the union of several states, provided the basis for construing the relations between state and federal governments upon principles of English common law, there were no such bases with respect to the tribes. To oversimplify the description of this situation, the consequence is that the United States has had to deal with Indians and their affairs through Anglo notions of its legal relations with them under the Constitution, affected by treaty provisions, court interpretations, and sovereign dominion; but, all of which are constrained by the acknowledged existence and exercise of residual sovereignty in the tribes that secures to them the right and power of regulating their internal affairs without foreign dictation.

Assuming that in the beginning tribes were absolute sovereigns, it might be broadly stated that these tribal sovereignties have been reduced to what they are today by interventions, or limitations upon them through treaties, through exercise of national sovereignty over them on the notion

Fig. 7.2 Certain offenses committed by Indians on reservations are tried before tribally appointed or elected judges. Judge William Roy Rhodes presiding over the tribal court in the Gila River Indian Community, 1972.

that conquest rendered the tribes subject to the power of the United States, and Congressional statutes and Executive actions implementing those treaties and powers derived from the Constitution. What remains has been described as internal sovereignty which provides the basis for self-government.

Treaty Interventions

Treaties were the accepted mode of dealing with the Indian tribes as independent nations during the colonial period extending into the first century under the Constitutional government. Then, by the Act of March 3, 1871,[3] Congress provided that "hereafter no Indian nation or tribe within the territory of the United States shall be acknowledged or recognized as an independent nation, tribe, or power with whom the United States may contract by treaty." It was not the intention of the enactment to invalidate or impair the obligations under treaties already made, although such treaties occupy the same status as other treaties having "domestic" application and are subject to be changed or revoked by later acts of Congress. Nor was it the intention of the act to do away with, or "extinguish," the existence of tribal status of Indians thus far recognized. Save as thus changed or revoked, these treaties continue to be the law of the land and are obligatory on Congress.

Notwithstanding the differences in these treaties in respect to their terms and conditions among the different tribes, the central objective was eventual "civilization" and "citizenship" for the Indians. To achieve this, it was necessary to cut off the power of the Indians to deal with other national powers on an independent basis as national entities and put them under exclusive control. This subjugation was accomplished even before the founding of the Republic through agreements made between the European nations claiming the right of acquisition of lands in the new world and decreeing that discovery would give the right to take such dominion. The principle thus established among the "discovering" nations of Europe was that discovery gave title to the government by whose subjects, or by whose authority, it was made.

The property notions of Europe read into this principle the nice distinctions between title which gave "lawful cause of entry into lands, whereof another is seized," and possession which another may have, but subject to the ultimate dominion of the title holder. It was possible then for the United States and its colonial predecessors to take title to the lands while yet occupied by the Indians. It is very doubtful that the Indians ever understood these distinctions, especially during the early period. In fact, the federal courts recognize the Indians' inability to understand the technicalities involved in dealings with the United States, by consistently acknowledging, although not always adhering to, the rule that treaties and statutes affecting the Indians are to be liberally construed, that doubtful expressions are to be resolved in favor of the Indians.[4]

Under these European property notions, the Indian was presumably not affected in his own concepts of ownership and could continue, undisturbed, enjoyment of his lands. In the landmark case of Johnson v. McIntosh, decided in 1823, the Supreme Court was faced with the question of whether the Indians could pass title to their land that was recognizable in the courts of the United States. The chiefs of the Illinois and Piankeshaw Nations had granted certain tracts of land to private individuals without acknowledgment from the government. Later, another grantee of lands within the same area, but whose grant was made by the government, claimed prior rights over the first grantee. Concluding that Indian tribes did not enjoy and could not convey complete title to the soil, the Court through Chief Justice Marshall gave an historic explanation of the discovery of the new world and how it should be acquired by the ambitious and enterprising European nations:

. . . the character and religion of its inhabitants afforded an apology for considering them as a people over whom the superior genius of Europe might claim an ascendency . . . . But, as they were all in pursuit of nearly the same object, it was necessary, in order to avoid conflicting settlements, and consequent war with each other, to establish a principle, which all should acknowledge as the law by which the right of acquisition, which they all asserted, should be regulated as between themselves . . . .
The exclusion of all other Europeans, necessarily gave to the nation making the discovery the sole right of acquiring the soil from the natives, and establishing settlements upon it. It was a right with which no Europeans could interfere . . . .
Those relations which were to exist between the discoverer and the natives, were to be regulated by themselves . . . .
In the establishments of these relations, the rights of the original inhabitants were, in no instance, entirely disregarded; but were necessarily, to a considerable extent, impaired. They were admitted to be the rightful occupants of the soil, with a legal as well as just claim to retain possession of it, and to use it according to their own discretion; but their rights to complete sovereignty, as independent nations, were necessarily diminished, and their power to dispose of the soil at their own will, to whomever they pleased, was denied by the original fundamental principle, that discovery gave exclusive title to those who made it.
While the different nations of Europe respected the right of the natives, as occupants, they asserted the ultimate dominion to be in themselves; and claimed and exercised, as a consequence of this ultimate dominion a power to grant the soil while yet in possession of the natives.
The United States, then, have unequivocally acceded to that great and broad rule by which its civilized inhabitants now hold this country. They hold, and assert in themselves, the title by which it was acquired . . . .
The power now possessed by the government of the United States

. . . has been exercised uniformly over territory in possession of the Indians. The existence of this power must negate the existence of any right which may conflict with and control it. An absolute title to lands cannot exist, at the same time, in different persons, or in different governments.[5]

Some years later, in 1832, the Court reached a conclusion that the Cherokee Nation, although holding their lands only under aboriginal right of occupancy and possession with the fee title in the United States, had such right as to preclude the State of Georgia from entering upon the Cherokee lands to enforce its laws without the consent of the Cherokee Nation. The Court acknowledged the title to be in the United States, not Georgia upon its claim under its colonial acquisition, and said the rule of acquisition did not affect the internal affairs of the Cherokee Nation, but gave exclusive right of dealing with the tribe to the national government.

It regulated the right given by discovery among the European discoverers; but could not affect the rights of those already in possession, either as aboriginal occupants, or as occupants by virtue of a discovery made before the memory of man . . . .
The United States succeeded to all claims of Great Britain, both territorial and political; but no attempt, so far as is known, has been made to enlarge them . . . .
. . . Great Britain . . . granted charters to companies of his subjects, who associated themselves for the purpose of carrying the views of the crown into effect . . . . They purport, generally, to convey the soil, from the Atlantic to the South Sea . . . The extravagant and absurd idea, that the feeble settlements made on the sea coast, or the companies under whom they were made, acquired legitimate power by them to govern the people, or occupy the lands from sea to sea, did not enter the mind of any man. They were well understood to convey the title which, according to the common-law of European sovereigns respecting America, they might rightfully convey, and no more. This was the exclusive right of purchasing such lands as the natives were willing to sell. The crown could not be understood to grant what the crown did not affect to claim; nor was it so understood.[6]

The Indians' right of aboriginal occupancy and communal use has been termed "Indian title" and was not a compensable property interest under the laws of the United States. Indeed, the courts were powerless to adjudicate claims concerning Indian title lands because they lacked jurisdiction to hear those claims. The extinguishment of Indian title by the sovereign act of the United States "has proceeded, as a political matter, without any admitted legal responsibility in the sovereign to compensate the Indian for his loss." However, Congress, through passage of the Indian Claims Commission Act on August 13, 1946,[7] has authorized tribes to sue the United States on the taking of original Indian title.

Thus, this principle of title by discovery which places the fee in the United States, and the notion of Indian title which recognizes only occupancy and use in the Indians, has a very important bearing on the Indians' exercise of self-government. As fee holder, the United States claims a right to intervene in any action which the tribe takes affecting this fee interest. Leases, rights of way, easements, and the like, all affect the fee and require approval from the fee owner as is also true with what is to be done with the rents, profits, or other incomes from them. Indian tribal governments, operating as they are in the nature of a municipality, are thus subjected to this imposition in no insignificant degree, when they make laws and ordinances dealing in uses of these lands for economic and other purposes.

Sovereign Intervention

It is said that the practical necessity, historically, of protecting the Indians, or defending against them, constituted a national problem which gave to the federal government exclusive power over Indians as against state power. Among the obligations historically assumed by the United States were ". . . to secure them in their title and possession of their lands, in the exercise of self-government, and to defend them from domestic strife and foreign enemies; and powers adequate to the fulfillment of those obligations are necessarily reserved."[8] With respect to securing them in their title and possession, the practical consideration was that if the federal government did not exercise exclusive right of dominion over the disposition of Indian title, individuals would deal directly with Indians for lands they were communally occupying, resulting in the displacement of Indians. The problems of resettling and compensating the Indians would fall on the sovereign or central government for solutions. And so, by virtue of this control over the fee with respect to its territories and possessions, the United States has exercised broad dominion and control over Indians who occupied lands within these territories and possessions. The Supreme Court in United States v. Kagama[9] likened the federal power over Indian tribes to the sovereign powers of Congress over the territories and their inhabitants:

But these Indians are within the geographical limits of the United States. The soil and the people within these limits are under the political control of the Government of the United States, or of the States of the Union. There exists within the broad domain of sovereignty but these two. There may be cities, counties, and other organized bodies with limited legislative functions, but they are all derived from, or exist in, subordination to one or the other of these. The territorial governments owe all their powers to the statutes of the United States conferring on them the powers which they exercise, and which are liable to be withdrawn, modified, or repealed at any time by Congress. . . . But this power of Congress to organize territorial governments, and make laws for their inhabitants, arises not so much from the clause in the Constitution in regard to disposing of and making rules and regulations concerning the Territory and other property of the United States, as from the ownership of the country in which the Territories are, and the right of exclusive sovereignty which must exist in the National Government, and can be found nowhere else . . . .

The power of the General Government over these remnants of a race once powerful, now weak and diminished in numbers, is necessary to their protection, as well as to the safety of those among whom they dwell. It must exist in that government because it has never existed anywhere else, because the theatre of its exercise is within the geographical limits of the United States, because it has never been denied, and because it alone can enforce its laws on all the tribes.

This sovereign exercise has sometimes been referred to as the plenary power of Congress over Indian tribes, and is also the basis for excluding state jurisdiction. Without this exercise, the tribes would have had extra-territoriality.

Indians are mentioned only once in the Constitution in the Commerce Clause wherein it states that Congress could regulate "commerce with . . . the Indian tribes." However, as already discussed, Congress exercises a much broader power than would be reasonably interpreted from this clause. Some of this broad interpretation has carried over from powers implied in other clauses which authorized Congress to treat the tribes as independent nations, and to exercise its war powers. In fact, Chief Justice Marshall maintained that the Constitutional powers of Congress to make war and peace, to make treaties, and to regulate commerce with Indian tribes comprehend all that is required for the regulation of intercourse with the Indians.[10]

While the Commerce Clause is the only grant of power in the Constitution which mentions Indians, that power plus the treaty making power is said to give a greater power over Indian tribes than the power over commerce between states. An opinion of the attorney general of the United States quoted with approval this statement:[11]

The purpose with which this power was given to Congress was not merely to prevent burdensome, conflicting or discriminating state legislation, but to prevent fraud, to protect an uncivilized people from wrongs by unscrupulous whites, and to guard the white population from the danger of savage outbreaks.

A grant made with such a purpose must convey a different power from one whose purpose was to insure the freedom of commerce. Congress has, in the case of the Indians, prohibited trade in certain articles, it has limited the right to trade to persons licensed under Federal laws, and in many ways asserted a greater control than would be possible over other branches of commerce.[12]

Numerous cases provide judicial statements supporting Congress's very wide power to manage and dispose of tribal lands. The interpretation of the Commerce Clause, against the background of treaties and sovereign relations with Indians resulting in tribal subordination in its relationship to lands, permits federal interventions to include not only matters over land, but also aspects of intercourse which have little or no relation to commerce — for example, travel, crimes by whites against Indians or Indians against whites, land survey, trespass and settlement by whites, fixing boundaries, and the furnishing of articles, services, and money by the federal government. Such broad interpretation has led to the evolvement of a trust relationship between the tribes and the federal government in the nature of guardian to his ward, whereby the federal government holds the land in fee title in trust for the Indians. In Morrison v. Work[13] the Court said:

It is admitted that, as regards tribal property subject to the control of the United States as guardian of Indians, Congress may make such changes in the management and disposition as it deems necessary to promote their welfare. The United States is now exercising, under the claim that the property is tribal, the powers of a guardian and of a trustee in possession.

Again the Court stated that:

Since the power of Congress over Indian affairs is plenary, it may waive or withdraw these duties of guardianship or entrust them to such agency — state or federal — as it chooses . . . .[14]

The duties of guardianship have been entrusted to a federal agency which is the Bureau of Indian Affairs operating under the rules and regulations of the secretary of the interior. However, the administrative execution of this trust has become a super-imposition over the exercise of Indian self-government such that tribal autonomy is difficult to glean from this imposition. One author describes it this way:

The reservation governments have had a shaky existence, suffering the whims of Congress and the overarching impositions of impolite bureaucrats from the Bureau of Indian Affairs. The tribal chairman, in all this, has often been something of a cog, a powerless representative with a seeming responsibility of leadership.[15]

In delegating this trust, Congress authorized the president to appoint, with the consent of the Senate, a commissioner of Indian affairs who was to have ". . . the direction and management of all Indian affairs, and of all matters arising out of Indian relations . . . ."[16] Then, with the Act of March 3, 1849,[17] Congress authorized the secretary of the interior to ". . . exercise the supervisory and appellate powers now exercised by the Secretary of the War Department, in relation to all the acts of the Commissioner of Indian Affairs."

Armed with this authority and power, the commissioner has in turn delegated these to the directors of regional areas and finally to agency superintendents within the Bureau of Indian Affairs. But Congressional statutes which are the source of this power, do not provide specifically for every possibility that may arise, consequently, the secretary has wide discretion to act in situations not so provided for as "guardian of all Indian interests."[18] Nevertheless, in his dealings with the Indians the secretary of the interior does not have "the power of an Asiatic potentate or even of a benevolent despot," but is subject to legislative restrictions.[19]

Among the important powers exercised by the secretary is the power to make rules and regulations intended to spell out the acts of Congress for better interpretation and enforcement, and this is well demonstrated by a wide range of regulations concerning Indians embodied in Title 25 of the Code of Federal Regulations. The administrative implementation of these regulations down through the network of bureaucracy gives substance to the statement that the Bureau of Indian Affairs seems to be a super-imposition over the tribal exercise of self-government. A noted expert in Indian law had this to say about this situation:

> But Indians for some decades have had neither armies nor lawyers to oppose increasingly broad interpretations of the power of the Commissioner of Indian Affairs, and so little by little, 'the management of all Indian affairs of the Federal Government' has come to be read as 'management of all the affairs of Indians' . . . .[20]

State Intervention

Because of its plenary control, Congress has precluded state intervention into tribal affairs except where it expressly grants authority to the state. This has not been interpreted to mean the states are precluded from *all* affairs on the Indian reservations, but, as tribes have begun to exercise their inherent powers in the context of modern day affairs, the delimitations of state and tribal jurisdictions have become a very complicated problem.

An example of a Congressional grant to states is the General Allotment Act which granted individual parcels of land to Indians and provided

that after the issuance of a patent in fee, the use and benefit of such allotments would be in accordance with the laws of the state or territory where
such land is located. Such state laws as "compulsory school attendance"
and "sanitation and quarantine regulations" may be authorized for enforcement on reservations "under such rules, regulations, and conditions
as the Secretary of the Interior may prescribe," but these have been
limited to those reservations where tribes have adopted their own laws
consenting to such application.

Then by the Act of August 15, 1953,[21] Congress gave consent to
states to remove "where necessary, constitutional or statutory impediments
in its laws to the assumption of criminal and civil jurisdictions in Indian
country." The impediment, in so far as Arizona is concerned, is incorporated in its constitution from the Enabling Act to its statehood where the
people agree and declare that they forever disclaim all right and title to
all lands owned and held by Indians within the state boundaries. Until
the Indian title to these lands is extinguished, they are to remain subject
to the disposition and absolute control of Congress. A later amendment,
embodied as a rider to the statute purporting to grant the bill of rights to
Indians, states that assumption by states of civil and criminal jurisdiction
over Indians requires the consent of the tribe. And although only Congress
is said to have the power to determine how and when Indian title may
be extinguished, it is not always without liability.

Much litigation has tested the principles underlying the exclusive
powers of the federal government over Indians as they have been earlier
expressed, and those principles have to this day been basically upheld
with some modifications in their interpretations. In Williams v. Lee,[22]
a case arising in Arizona, the court said the question of state action regarding tribal affairs was whether it infringed on the rights of reservation
Indians to make their own laws and be ruled by them. In this case, a non-
Indian trader on the Navajo Reservation sought in the Arizona courts to
enforce collection for goods sold on credit to Indians on the reservation.

In another Arizona case the Court, in striking down Arizona tax as
applied to a federally-licensed Indian trader on the Navajo Reservation,
reasoned that this imposition, in addition to those Congress or the tribe
have prescribed, would "disturb and disarrange the statutory plan" of
Congress to protect the Indians.[23] These cases also recognize that state
action might be possible in areas where essential tribal relations were not
involved and where the rights of Indians would not be jeopardized. But,
what are essential tribal relations is said to be for Congress alone to
determine, and not the courts. Moreover, Congress is bound by high
standards of fair dealings in respect to any action it takes affecting Indians.

State interventions, then, are as much to be guided by principles which recognize the tribal right of self-government as federal interventions, and this is not less so because some tribal governments are not sophisticated in the management of their affairs. This unsophistication is no reason, by itself, for intervention with substitute laws. A legal opinion stated by the solicitor for the Department of Interior said that it

... is a fact that State governments and administrative officials have frequently trespassed upon the realm of tribal autonomy, presuming to govern the Indian tribes through State law or departmental regulation or arbitrary administrative fiat, but these trespasses have not impaired the vested legal powers of local self-government which have been recognized again and again when these trespasses have been challenged by an Indian tribe.[24]

And so, throughout the history of dealings with Indians and Indian tribes, administrative officials, both state and federal, have been forced to reckon with the doctrine of Indian right of self-government.

The high water mark of legislative recognition of this doctrine was the Indian Reorganization Act mentioned earlier, sometimes referred to as the Wheeler-Howard Act of 1934. This act provides that the Indian tribe which organizes under its provisions can adopt a constitution approved by the secretary of the interior. Section 16 of this act states that "in addition to all powers vested in any Indian tribe or tribal council by existing law, the constitution adopted by said tribe shall also vest" enumerated powers. The Arizona tribal constitutions follow the same basic pattern in setting out jurisdiction, membership, organization, and powers of tribal councils, amendment provisions, and in naming what aspects of tribal actions would be subject to review by the secretary of the interior. The similarities are explainable by the fact that, at the time these constitutions were under consideration by the tribes, they were almost totally the subjects of agency superintendency, and it was necessary for the BIA to provide a format by which the tribes could take the initiative and which format, undoubtedly, became available to all.

The question of whether these constitutions are grants of power and authority from Congress, and operate as extinguishment of tribal sovereignty, or whether they have preserved it, was answered by the solicitor of the Department of the Interior when he interpreted the clause "powers vested in any Indian tribe or tribal council by existing law" contained in the Indian Reorganization Act:

Perhaps the most basic principle of all Indian law, supported by a host of decisions hereinafter analyzed, is the principle that those powers which are lawfully vested in an Indian tribe are not, in general, delegated powers granted by express acts of Congress, but rather inherent powers of a limited sovereignty which has never been extinguished. Each Indian tribe begins its relationship with the Federal Government as a sovereign power, recognized as such in treaty and legislation. The powers of sovereignty have been limited from time to time by special treaties and laws designed to take from the Indian tribes control of matters which, in the judgment of Congress, these tribes could no longer be safely permitted to handle. The statutes of Congress, then, must be examined to determine the limitations of tribal sovereignty rather than to determine its sources or its positive content. What is not expressly limited remains within the domain of tribal sovereignty, and therefore properly falls within the statutory category, 'powers vested in any Indian tribe or tribal council by existing law.'[25]

Another fundamental principle of law is that power and authority rightfully conferred do not necessarily cease to exist in consequence of long nonuse. Under this concept the Indian Reorganization Act is seen as statutory recognition of these powers of self-government and only affords administrative assistance in developing the mechanisms by which such tribal governments may act. These actions, in turn, may alleviate the conditions which have often been seen as justification for agencies of the federal and state governments to intervene in matters that were properly within the legal competence of the Indian tribes themselves.

8. Living Conditions

Gordon V. Krutz

SINCE THE LATE 1800s, there have been numerous attempts to improve the living conditions of Arizona Indians which have lagged far behind those of non-Indians in a rapidly expanding economy. This lag is manifested in all phases of community development, such as industrial development, small business enterprises, housing, and employment opportunities. Only recently are incipient phases of business and industrial development beginning to dot the landscape on some Arizona Indian reservations. A suggested reason for this lag is the difference which exists between Indian and dominant society goals. In the past eighty years these Indian goals have not been considered in the development plans superimposed upon them. It is not unreasonable, therefore, to expect an unwillingness on the part of the Indian to support such programs.

An additional hypothesis for explaining the Indian's behavior in this area may be that the greater the pressure for Indian development by the dominant society *without Indian involvement,* the greater will be the Indian's resistance.

In order to understand this phenomenon, it is necessary to examine the historical relationship between the federal government and individual tribal groups. After Indian reservations were established in the nineteenth century, there was a serious federal effort to mold American Indian behavior after the dominant society which it was assumed could serve as an ideal model to guide the Indian in his social and economic development. However, this did not prove to be the case; Indians resisted the superimposition of a model without their direct involvement. Development programs for the Indian community were the products of federal agents who were outside the Indian system. This process of doing things for, and not with Indians, resulted in the development of a dependency role between the Indian community and the federal government. Such change programs were identified by the Indian community as lying outside the realm of tribal interest and support.

Fig. 8.1   While stainless steel and "modernized" cooking prevail in many areas such as this BIA school cafeteria, the traditional methods of preparation still have an attraction of their own and are featured on such occasions as this fiesta.

In addition the displacement of native authority by the federal agent and the dependency on outside energy to develop the Indian community has resulted in the Indians' unwillingness to become involved with improvement programs. The process of eighty years of dependency relations between the tribes and the federal government is, thus, directly related to the developmental lag in Arizona Indian communities. It should be mentioned that this situation did not prevail prior to contact with the white man, when Arizona Indians were self-sufficient farmers, hunters, and gatherers, as has been indicated in chapter two.

Federal agencies are beginning to recognize past failures in program development which excludes Indian involvement and are trying to rectify this oversight by establishing new programs to inspire Indian self-determination. Basic to the philosophy of self-determination, which has the support of President Nixon, is the revitalization of native initiative. This initiative is being encouraged by the federal government by contracting with tribal groups for services formerly provided by the federal government. These contracts place Indian leaders in a position to plan for and develop their own communities according to the needs dictated by their own value systems. Presently only the Zuñi tribe in New Mexico has contracted for the management of federal services to their community. It is too early to evaluate the ultimate effect of such a plan.

The basic living conditions which underlie the poor economic development of Arizona Indian communities should be discussed to alert the reader to plans for improvement.

Housing, Sanitation, Water

From a 1970 survey by the Indian Health Service in Phoenix, of 5,694 homes, involving some 29,284 Indians,[1] and from a 1970 report of 8,600 Indian homes by the Bureau of Indian Affairs, Phoenix,[2] a basic profile can be presented of the condition of Indian homes, sanitation, and water supplies.

Nearly half of all Indian homes, reported in the IHS 1970 survey, are of wood-frame construction. Another 20 percent are of adobe construction, 20 percent of masonry, and the remainder are trailers, and of log, sod, and other construction. The average Indian family of 5.1 persons lives in a house with four or less rooms; only 4 percent of the families live in houses with more than six rooms. Almost two-thirds of the families live in houses with less than six hundred square feet, while one-fifth of the families live in homes larger than eight hundred square feet (this figure reflects the number of self-help housing). Approximately 25 percent of all

Fig. 8.2   A Navajo hogan with Shiprock in the distance.

homes inspected in the IHS 1970 survey need some form of repair: broken
windows, doors, walls, and holes in roofs. The Bureau of Indian Affairs'
1970 survey stated that 67 percent of the 8,600 houses need replace-
ment, 17 percent require renovation, and only 16 percent are considered adequate.

Slightly over half of the homes in the Indian Health Service's survey
have running water, a sink in the kitchen and a sanitary waste system.
Only 25 percent of the homes have bath facilities and nearly two-thirds
of the families are without flush toilets. However, the survey indicates
that 70 percent of the homes use electricity and 60 percent have refrigera-
tors. Unfortunately, there are no data for radio and television sets, an
indicator of off-reservation communication, although TV antennas wherever reception is possible, are apparent in many Indian communities and
many Indian youths carry transistor radios.

In short, the surveys show that the average Arizona Indian has five
members in his family, lives in a wood frame house of four rooms or
less, with under 600 square feet in area, uses electricity, owns a refrigerator and television set, has running water, a kitchen sink, an outdoor
privy, and lacks thermostatically controlled heating.

Available Services

The three federal agencies responsible for housing, water, and sanitation in Arizona Indian communities are the Bureau of Indian Affairs (BIA), the Indian Health Service (IHS), and the Housing and Urban Development Department (HUD).

The Indian Health Service assumed responsibility for health care from the BIA in 1955. In 1959 Congress passed Public Law 86-121 to provide funds for the improvement of basic water and sanitation facilities on American Indian reservations. This program enabled the IHS, at the request of the tribe, to provide basic materials and supervision for installing water and sanitation systems, with the tribe agreeing to provide land and labor for the installation and to assume its management after completion. The IHS also agrees to provide training for Indian crews for the maintenance and operation of the system. This agreement usually results in tribal organization of utility committees, not only to operate and maintain the water sanitation system, but to collect water fees, and plan for expanded services.

In 1970, better than half of the Indian families of Phoenix area jurisdiction have running water in their homes, although 60 percent of all the area's families still use outdoor privies.[3] The PL 86-121 program has stimulated many families to construct additions to their homes for housing a kitchen sink, flush toilet, and wash basin, and to remodel their homes completely to match the new improvements. One of the most important aspects of this program has been the installation of septic tanks and flush toilets which provide for the sanitary disposal of human waste matter, thus helping to curb the spread of infectious diseases by controlling flying and crawling insects.

The Indian Health Service will place 90 percent of the PL 86-121 budget for the 1971 fiscal year into new housing programs in cooperation with the BIA and HUD. With this additional construction and planned improvements through other programs by 1975, the need for sound housing will be reduced from 84 percent in 1969 to 36 percent in 1975.[4]

There are many combinations of housing construction programs available to the Indian family; generally they provide for a modern three or four bedroom house with bath, indoor plumbing, and regulated temperature control. At the present time there are three types of housing programs financed jointly by BIA and HUD: Mutual Self-Help, Low Rent, and Turnkey.

In general, the Mutual Self-Help Program requires a minimum of 10 percent sweat equity during the construction of the home by the participant with Housing Assistant Administration (HAA) providing the remainder of

Fig. 8.3   A Papago man making adobe bricks on the reservation west of Tucson.

the construction capital. Payments for the homes are based on the participant's income, but in no case will it exceed 25 percent of the participant's
gross income, including utilities. The Low Rent Program is a program whereby
the Local Housing Authority has a housing project built with HAA funding
which the Local Housing Authority owns and operates as rental properties.
The Turnkey Program is constructed by a contractor and sold to the Local
Housing Authority and then sold to the individual family.[5]

In sum, the federal agencies dealing with Indian housing, water, and
sanitation have been steadily improving these basic living conditions
through a series of programs. An important factor in these programs is

118   LIVING CONDITIONS

TABLE 8.1

The Leading Five Notifiable Diseases for the Calendar Year 1969

Diseases	Peak Year	No. Cases	Low Year	No. Cases
1. Inner Ear Infection (Otitis Media)	1969	4314	1967	3422
2. Gastroenteritis	1966	4598	1968	3810
3. Pneumonia	1966	2520	1969	1482
4. Trachoma	1966	3166	1969	1180
5. Streptococcus Throat Infection	1969	793	1965	288

Source: Phoenix Area Indian Health Service, *Reported New Cases of Notifiable Diseases,* Annual Report, 1969.

that by contracting with federal agencies the tribes are organizing water and sanitation committees and local housing authorities and are becoming involved with community planning; all such activities encourage Indian self-determination.

Health Conditions

The most prevalent major diseases in Arizona Indian communities are listed in Table 8.1.

The picture of communicable diseases in Indian communities can be seen in better perspective when compared with the general U.S. population. This is shown in Table 8.2 which uses the Navajo as representative of the Arizona Indian population for comparative purposes.

Tuberculosis and hepatitis occur over 7½ times, streptococcus infection, over 34 times, and rheumatic fever almost 119 times more frequently among the Navajo than in the general U.S. population.

The Indian Health Service summarized the implications of these statistics in the following manner:

High on the list of health problems are those infectious diseases associated with poor home conditions and the harsh physical environment, and where there is unsafe and poor supply of water, poor and crowded housing conditions, unsanitary waste disposal and lack of insect control. Improper food handling and lack of refrigeration contribute to the high incidence of gastrointestinal disease.[6]

Communicable diseases directly related to poor sanitary conditions such as gastroenteritis and trachoma have been reduced since 1966, per-

TABLE 8.2

Incidence of Diseases Among the Navajo
Compared to the U.S. Population

Disease	Navajo Incidence Per 100,000 Population	General Population U.S. Incidence Per 100,000 Population
Tuberculosis	175	23
Rheumatic Fever	237	2
Streptococcus Throat Infection	7,861	229
Hepatitis	161	21
Pneumonia	4,697	Not Reported
Acute Otitis Media	13,611	Not Reported
Gastroenteritis	9,583	Not Reported
Trachoma	1,583	Not Reported

Source: Navajo Area Indian Health Service, Health Problems, Health Programs, Health Program Deficiencies and Justification for Increased Fiscal Year 1971 Resources, prepared at request of the Navajo tribe, 1970.

haps, reflecting improved on-reservation sanitation systems, whereas diseases, related to poor housing, crowded living conditions, and uncontrolled indoor heating, such as streptococcus infections have increased.

Malnutrition

Malnutrition is a problem directly associated with low income and poor living conditions. A five-year study of malnutrition in Navajo Head Start children for the period 1963-1967, reported the relationship of malnutrition to disease spread.

In the 5-year period of study there were 4355 admissions to the pediatric service of children under 5 years of age. Of the total number, 616 had diagnoses of malnutrition. Forty-four had diagnoses of the severest malnutrition, (of which) 15 had Kwashiorkor and 29 had Marasmus. Nearly 15% of all pediatric admissions during the time period 1963 through 1967 had some form of associated malnutrition. In addition the height and weight of the Head Start Navajo children from all over the reservation were below the Iowa-Boston norms. This is probably the end result of chronic calorie and protein malnutrition acting in synergism with repeated bacterial and viral infections, causing repeated episodes of gastroenteritis and respiratory infections and contributing to increased infant mortality.[7]

Health Service Agencies

The Arizona State Health Department and the Indian Health Service, Division of the U.S. Public Health Service are the two primary agencies concerned with the health problems of Arizona Indians. The State Health Department provided the following health care services amounting to $109,097.79 for fiscal years 1968 and 1969: cooperation with the Chinle Nursing Home on the Navajo reservation; review and approval by the Water Pollution Control Division of six applications for PL 660 funds for Indian projects; advice and consultation in nutritional programs, school nursing services, and vision and hearing screening programs; tuberculosis control by providing a TB register, laboratory services, skin testing programs, mobile X-ray facilities and services in the State Tuberculosis Sanatorium; venereal disease control, and other epidemiologic services.[8]

The Division of Indian Health is divided into jurisdictions under the Phoenix and Navajo area offices, each of which has its own major hospital facility. These two areas are sub-divided into service units, each having a unit hospital, medical staff, and field health staff. The Phoenix area has seven service units located at Keams Canyon, Parker, Phoenix, Sacaton, San Carlos, and Whiteriver; the Navajo area in Arizona has three service units located at Fort Defiance, Tuba City, and Winslow. In addition to direct hospital care, the IHS has programs in dental care, TB control, trachoma control, nutrition, family planning, mental health, and sanitation.

Impressive improvements have been made in the health care of Arizona Indians since 1955. However, there are limitations to the services offered through such health programs. This is not to say that health services are poor, quite the contrary, health services to Arizona Indians are among the very best in the nation. But limits are set by a restrictive environment which includes such factors as poor housing, unemployment, underemployment, and poor attitudes toward health care. The availability of good health facilities does not mean that a community will utilize them. This problem indicates the great need for health education through the native employee, stated in a special way to motivate the individual to use modern health care as an alternate or in addition to native treatment of ill health and prevention of disease.

Community Health Representatives

Recently, the IHS has initiated an innovative program to involve Indians in planning health programs, in controlling communicable diseases and in reaching community members who fail to utilize modern

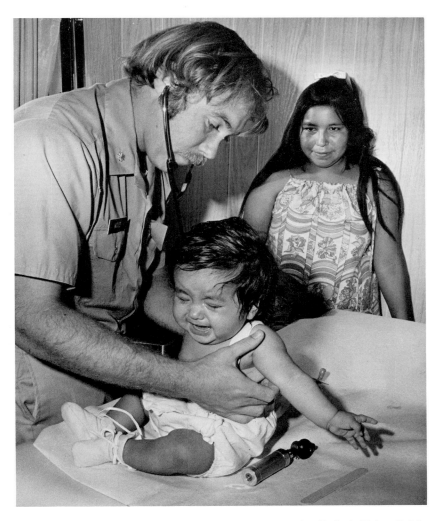

Fig. 8.4 A physician examines a reluctant baby at the United States Public Health Service Hospital in the Gila River Indian Community.

Fig. 8.5   A Papago family harvesting fruit from the saguaro, one of several native foods used as traditional supplements to modern diets in many parts of the state.

health facilities. The Community Health Representative Program employs native speaking members of the community in a tribal-IHS contract to serve as liaison between the community and the health staff. The health representative is a tribal employee, chosen by the people of his own community and trained to work with basic community health problems. His prime tasks are:

1. Alerting his community to health problems and the availability of health services.
2. Assisting families in improving and maintaining good health.
3. Conducting surveys and gathering vital statistics.
4. Interpreting to the families the environmental conditions which need change to improve their health and serving as an advisor in planning health programs.
5. Referring individuals to health personnel and following through to insure that the prescribed instructions and appointments are kept.
6. Assisting patients with emergency transportation for health services.[9]

The CHR Program is one step in the direction of Indian self-determination in health care. Another step is in the operation of tribal health committees which work with both on- and off-reservation health problems. On-reservation health committees are appointed by the tribal council and serve as advisors to the local medical staff and tribal council. Off-reservation health committees serve as advisory boards to the IHS area staff in defining long-range health plans.

Other innovative health programs are found in the fields of analysis and training. The IHS operates the Health Programs System Center at San Xavier which is developing a massive communication system to make possible the instant retrieval of medical data on individual patients to facilitate the prescription of proper medication and therapy. They also work with health models, using computer science to trace disease patterns and to prescribe corrective action. The IHS has a center at Tucson which serves as a conference and training site for IHS and CHR personnel.

Even with the best medication available it is difficult to prevent the spread of upper respiratory infections and other contagious diseases in a population living under crowded conditions, in poorly heated houses, with unsafe water, poor sanitation, and exposed to invading insects. These living conditions can be improved by programs which offer modern houses and utilities, but unless the individual can afford to purchase such housing, backed by steady employment, he will hesitate to enter into an agreement obligating him to a long-term contract.

9. Employment, Economic Development, and Assistance Programs

Gordon V. Krutz

Employment

THE ECONOMIC WELL-BEING of Arizona Indian communities should be of primary concern to all Arizona citizens since changes within these communities will reflect and influence changes within the total economic structure of the state. Arizona Indian communities encompass 26 percent of the state's total land area, much of which includes prime recreation areas and mineral deposits. In the field of economic development it is essential to maintain good state and tribal relations since tribal developments, not subject to state control, could seriously affect the lives of all Arizona citizens.

The rate of Indian population growth is impressive and needs to be considered as an important variable in the planning of Arizona's future. For example, the Navajo tribe's population of 40,000 in 1941 has grown to an estimated 120,000 in 1970. Another factor for consideration is that many Arizona Indians maintain both on- and off-reservation homes, many thousands of Indians live and work in our urban areas, attend public schools, pay taxes, and vote in elections. In some counties the Indian population represents a majority: Apache County is 76.43 percent, Navajo 49.33 percent, and Gila 15.25 percent Indian.[1] The rapid growth of Arizona Indian tribes is becoming a serious factor in the state's economic picture. Successful Indian employment could mean a better life for all Arizonans.

Unemployment

The BIA reported in 1970 an Indian work force of 13,607, excluding the Navajo. Of this available work force, 47.5 percent is permanently employed, 19.9 percent temporarily employed, and 32.6 percent unemployed.[2] The reported work force for the Navajo Reservation as a whole, which includes parts of other states, is 39,363. Of the available work force for the Navajo, 30 percent are permanently employed, 26.7 percent are temporarily employed, and 43.3 percent are unemployed. A recent study of the economic conditions of three Arizona reservations, shows that over half of the families have annual incomes of less than $3,000 which contrasts sharply with the average for the United States of $6,882 for 1967. The study indicated that the average income ranged from $500-$999 for the Fort Apaches and Papagos, and the median family income for the San Carlos was in the $1,000-$1,999 range.[3]

The data indicate that Arizona Indian communities lag far behind the economic advances of Arizona non-Indian communities. It would seem difficult, indeed, to maintain a family of five with an annual income of less than $3,000, especially if the family head has only a 50 percent chance for employment. One might suggest that the Indian has the alternative of off-reservation employment. But does he really have this alternative, considering his close cultural and family ties which would be jeopardized by accepting employment at some distant place? While there are approximately 22,000 Indians living off the reservations, a figure which represents less than 12 percent of the total Arizona Indian population, many of these people still think of the reservation as "home." It is mandatory, therefore, to consider seriously the continued support of economic development on all reservations.

Off-Reservation Employment Opportunities

Employment opportunities are available to Arizona Indians off-reservation and on-reservation. In off-reservation employment the Indian competes in the same manner in the job market as any other American citizen. His level of employment is directly related to past experience, attitude, performance, educational training, production records, and conformance to time schedules. The Indian holding steady employment must learn the work habits of the dominant society. This society has little tolerance for tardiness, absenteeism, and erratic performance patterns. Furthermore, the employee is expected to serve as a team member and be responsive to supervision and loyal to the employer.

Employment values such as longevity, productivity, and performance often conflict with Indian values which oppose tight time schedules and the acquisition of wealth beyond immediate needs. Often, too, the Indians' religious and ceremonial calendar does not correspond to the standard holiday schedule, causing a conflict between loyalty to the job and Indian culture. Generally, a commitment to steady employment within the dominant system could result in two alternatives: a rejection of Indian values in favor of the values of the dominant society, or a compartmentalization of work patterns while on the job, retaining Indian identity off the job.

TABLE 9.1

Indian Placements in the State of Arizona by Industry 1965-1969

Industry	1965	1966	1967	1968	1969
Mining	93	61	57	60	179
Contract Construction	435	530	612	928	815
Manufacturing	844	621	988	1220	1512
Transportation, Commercial and Public Utilities	133	164	150	162	222
Trade	1906	2282	2310	2842	3092
Services	3865	1692	1784	1796	1907
Private Household	4411	4803	4795	5084	4746
Government	1512	2428	2035	1319	960
Other	232	236	196	279	253
Total Non-Agriculture	13,431	12,817	12,927	13,690	13,686
Total Agriculture	15,310	12,447	8,074	9,633	6,726
TOTAL	28,741	25,264	21,001	23,323	20,412

Sources: Manpower Services to Arizona Indians 1969, Arizona State Employment Service, June 1970, Phoenix.

Whatever the employment adjustment mechanisms are in the dominant system there seems to be little tolerance for the Indian system. The Indian employee either adjusts to the system or he is forced out!

However, in spite of adjustment problems and cross-cultural conflicts, Arizona Indians are successfully holding off-reservation employment. In 1969 the Arizona State Employment Service (ASES) placed 20,412 Indians, of which 13,686 were in non-agricultural employment.[4] In an effort to train the Indian workman, the ASES, in cooperation with the federal government, recruits trainees through the Manpower Development and Training Act (MDTA). A total of 295 Indians entered MDTA programs in Arizona during fiscal year 1970. The ASES also provides testing and counseling services to Arizona Indians; in 1969 the ASES administered 2,208 aptitude and proficiency tests and conducted 677 counseling interviews with Indians. Table 9.1 shows Indian placements by the ASES over a five-year period.

Off-reservation employment services to Arizona Indians are also provided by the BIA through the Employment Assistance Program, offering direct employment, vocational guidance and counseling, and adult vocational on-the-job and apprenticeship training. The majority of Ari-

Fig. 9.1 An alternative to off-reservation employment is the development of Indian arts and crafts. Top, young Hopi girl watches her grandmother weaving a basket, which will either be sold directly or through a trading post or off-reservation merchant. Left, a Navajo woman splits straw into three strips for basket weaving. Right, a rug weaving demonstration at the Navajo Tribal Museum in Window Rock. Bottom, the late Ida Redbird displays her Maricopa Indian pottery.

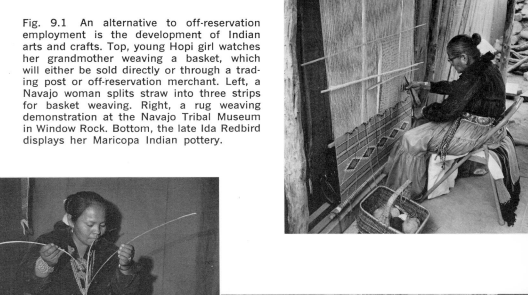

zona Indians have received institutional training in Phoenix, Oakland, and Los Angeles. During fiscal year 1969, 894 Arizona Indians entered adult vocational training of which 113 were trained in Arizona; a total of 399 were placed in on-the-job training projects in Arizona.[5] Other opportunities for learning job skills are available at the Chandler Career Center, and two skill centers at Sacaton and San Carlos. The Chandler Center is operated under a contract with the U.S. Department of Labor awarded to a non-profit consortium of local businessmen known as Creative Localism, Inc. The skill centers operate under a similar contract from the Labor Department under direct supervision from the community colleges at Coolidge and Thatcher.

Off-reservation employment services are also provided by the Phoenix and Tucson Indian centers. The Phoenix Indian Center reported 3,703 contacts for service information and referrals during a seven-month period in 1969. Of this total, 166 Indian workers were placed on the job.[6] The Indian center also provides services in counseling and guidance, referrals for health care, legal services, and an alcoholic rehabilitation program.

Reservation Employment and Economic Development

Serious attempts were made to terminate federal services to American Indian communities during the Eisenhower administration. Concerned over rising administration costs of Indian services and the slow rate at which Indian communities were developing, the BIA instituted a program to assimilate Indians into the mainstream of American society. This program was successful in the termination of nine Indian reservations. Each of these reservations experienced varying degrees of socioeconomic disaster, a factor which has caused the development of suspicion of federal motives in any new program which portends of termination.

It appears that termination continues to receive little Indian support. They see it as a direct threat to their religious and cultural associations and to the extinction of their land rights and even themselves as a people. Since the Indians have refused to terminate ownership of their lands and to assimilate into the mainstream, the federal government has reversed its plans in favor of developing reservation human and natural resources. This new federal program recognizes the right of the American Indian to determine his own future and to have a direct hand in the development of his resources.

In an effort to facilitate the philosophy of Indian self-determination, many new programs aimed at Indian economic development have proliferated: the Office of Economic Opportunity (OEO), the Industrial Development Branch of the BIA, the Economic Development Adminis-

Fig. 9.2   Loans from various sources such as the Indian Development District of Arizona and the Small Business Administration helped establish this canvas factory in the Gila River Indian Community.

tration (EDA), the Small Business Administration (SBA), and the Indian Development District of Arizona (IDDA). Each of these organizations is promoting economic changes on Indian reservations. For example, the BIA, in an effort to encourage industries to locate on or near reservations, serves as the coordinating agent between the industrial firm, federal funding, and the tribe. These efforts are reflected in the establishment of industrial parks as sites for industrial development on or near the following reservations: Gila River, San Carlos, Navajo, San Xavier, and Colorado River. As an inducement for the location of an industrial firm on an Indian reservation, a twenty-five-year lease may be obtained at $500 a year per acre with special tax advantages, and in some cases funding up to 80 percent of the building costs is absorbed through an EDA Grant. A summary of EDA funding for Arizona Indian reservations is found in Table 9.2.

TABLE 9.2

EDA Approved Projects for Arizona Indian Reservations

September 1969	
Grants	$ 7,470,000
Public Works	3,796,000
Loans	2,009,000
Business Loans	2,223,000
Planning Grants	75,000
Technical Assistance	321,000
Indian Development District of Arizona	189,000
Indian Tribes of Arizona, Inc.	10,000
Total Arizona EDA Projects	$16,093,000

Source: Manpower Services to Arizona Indians 1969, Arizona State Employment Service, June 1970, Phoenix.

The Small Business Administration has made loans to Indians in Arizona, most of them for reservation enterprises. By early 1970, the SBA had approved twenty-six loans for Indian businesses amounting to over $400,000, providing for the employment of seventy-eight Indians.

The Indian Development District of Arizona (IDDA) was started in 1967 to aid sound economic planning and development on member reservations. Its membership is composed of fifteen Arizona reservations. A state-chartered nonprofit corporation, IDDA attempts to unite tribal effort and an effective association with non-Indian communities in coordinating economic development efforts. IDDA personnel are accountable to an Indian board representing fifteen Arizona reservations.

Other reservation employment is found in tribal enterprises, federal and state employment, and with such private firms as timber and mining. The ASES maintains ten on-reservation branch offices, staffed with fourteen Indian employees who are native speakers.

Welfare

The payment of welfare and related social and political ills have become a major problem which affects the very fabric of American society. Within a short time span of about twenty years welfare payments have become a sizeable portion of state and federal budgets. Many believe that it is difficult for a society that places a high value on individual self-sufficiency to justify welfare as a real social need, but for many citizens welfare constitutes the only means for survival. In spite of serious efforts to eradicate welfare as an economic ill, a proportion of our society still lives under conditions of severe underemployment and unemployment and requires some form of assistance. Also included are the disabled, the aged, the handicapped and those with dependent children who are unable to care for them. The welfare needs of Arizona Indians are served by both the state welfare department and the social service branch of the BIA.

State Welfare Services

A report from the Arizona State Department of Public Welfare for fiscal year 1969-70 shows that a monthly average of 6,642 Indians received some form of welfare payment. These payments in the form of old age assistance went to 2,371 recipients, while 2,768 families received aid to dependent children grants for 9,072 children. There were payments to 1,342 permanently and totally disabled persons, and 161 received aid to the blind grants. The annual expenditures in these programs amounted to $6,587,464, with an average of $548,955 for each month.[7] These figures include monies received from the BIA and other federal agencies.

The state welfare department assists with the distribution of surplus food commodities to Arizona Indian reservations. During fiscal year 1969-70 a total of 9,537,021 pounds of surplus food commodities were distributed to an average of 35,441 persons each month with an aggregate value of $3,571,400.92 for the year.[8]

The division of child welfare services works closely with the BIA in the placement and supervision of Indian children in foster homes. The BIA provides the financial support for this program, which placed 215 reservation children during fiscal year 1969-70. In addition, 84 reservation children were placed in adoptive homes from July 1, 1968, through June 30, 1970.[9]

BIA Welfare Services

The objective of the BIA's program in social services is to help the Indian to develop a higher standard of living, a feeling of greater individual worth and a greater capacity to function as a member of the community and the family, utilizing resources of the group or individual, social agencies of the state, both public and private, and direct services of the bureau. The welfare program administered by the BIA for the Phoenix area is quoted below with some modifications from a 1969 report.

"The program of social services undertakes to provide necessary assistance and social services for Indians on reservations when such assistance and services are not available through State or local public welfare agencies. It is the general position of the Bureau that insofar as possible Indians should have the same relationship to public welfare as non-Indians, and that public welfare agencies should have the same responsibility for providing services and assistance as they have for non-Indians in similar circumstances. It is recognized, however, that there are certain services required by some Indians which are not provided by the State and local welfare agencies, and the tax-exempt status of Indian lands may affect the ability of the State or local government to meet the needs of Indians, particularly if Indians constitute a considerable portion of their population.

"Bureau responsibility for social services and related activities differ somewhat on different reservations, depending upon economic conditions on reservations, the availability of tribal resources, the responsibilities assumed by State or local welfare agencies, differences in local customs and attitudes, and the degree to which tribal institutions and controls are effective. Within the limits of its resources, the primary objectives of the Bureau's program of social services are: (1) to provide financial assistance (called general assistance) to needy Indian families living on reservations when employment is not available and when such assistance is not available from other sources; (this includes assisting interested Indian tribes to sponsor tribal work projects for recipients of assistance); (2) to provide counsel and guidance to Indians with family problems or other serious social problems; (3) to provide child welfare services when such services are not available from established child welfare agencies, including arrangements for the protection and care of dependent, neglected, and handicapped children, planning for adoption, and securing appropriate institutional care; (4) to interpret the social needs of Indian families and children to tribal governing bodies and tribal courts and provide assistance, when necessary and appropriate, in the development of tribal programs to meet those needs; (5) to provide information and liaison assistance to Indians to enable them to secure needed welfare services and assistance from State and local welfare programs for which they may be eligible; (6) to provide advice and counsel to Indians, when necessary, in planning constructive use of their own and their children's funds; and (7) to interpret the needs of Indians to community agencies and leaders away from the reservations and promote the acceptance of Indians on an equal basis with non-Indians.

"General assistance is provided directly by the Bureau when need has been determined. The same budgetary standards used by the State welfare agency for State public assistance programs are used to determine the individual's or family's general assistance needs. Provision is also made for care for Indians requiring care in institutions or nursing homes . . . .

"Most child welfare assistance and services are provided directly by the Bureau, but in addition, the Bureau has contracts with the State Welfare Department of Arizona for the provision of foster care to Indian children. This includes foster home finding, the placement of children in foster homes when living in their own homes is not possible or desirable, identification of handicapped Indian children in need of special care and arrangements for such care, and provisions of services and consultation to tribal courts so as to assist them in carrying out more effectively their legal responsibilities for the protection and care of Indian children . . . .

"Social Services, including counseling and guidance, are provided to recipients of general assistance and child welfare services, and also to other Indians with serious social problems which prevent them from functioning effectively. The purpose is to encourage and assist in efforts toward self-support, to promote more stable family life and improved parental care, to help Indians to recognize and cope with their social problems realistically, and to provide information about, and help Indians to use, other programs and resources which may be available. It must be admitted that it has not been possible to provide sufficient and adequate counseling and guidance services because, with the insufficient number of social work staff, case loads have been too high to permit the degree of individualized attention necessary.

"In addition to the responsibilities referred to above, Bureau social services staff perform other duties related to helping people. These include the important responsibility of recommending for or against approval of applications for Bureau boarding school when the application is based upon social rather than educational reasons; providing information and counseling regarding the availability of family planning services; assisting tribes, when necessary, to provide distribution of surplus food commodities on the reservation; assisting, when necessary, in the development of family plans for use of funds on reservations which have received awards of substantial judgment funds; assisting, when necessary, in the selection of eligible Indians in connection with Bureau housing programs; and cooperating with various activities of the Anti-poverty Programs under the Economic Opportunity Act.

"One innovation of the Bureau's program of social services has been the development, under joint sponsorship with the Child Welfare League of America, of the Indian Adoption Project. Under this Project homeless

Indian children, for whom adoptive homes are not available in the State of their residence, are referred through a central project office to reputable adoptive agencies in other States to be placed in adoptive homes . . . ."[10]

The Social Service Branch of the Phoenix Area Office of the Bureau of Indian Affairs provided assistance to an average of 4,320 Indians per month for fiscal year 1970; general assistance expenditures amounted to $2,004,978. The bureau also provided care for 622 children in foster homes or institutions at a cost of $69,373; child welfare expenditures amounted to $777,492.[11]

Tribal Work Experience Programs

The BIA in the Phoenix area has used general assistance funds to establish a rehabilitative program to prepare Indian workmen for employment. This tribal work experience program has opened up new areas for Indian employment. It is reported in full below from a release from the Indian Commissioner's office.

Gila River Program

"In the past three years the Gila River Indian Community, located south of Phoenix, Arizona, has been engaged in an extensive development program involving economic, social, community, and governmental activities. These programs are part of their VH-THAW-HUP-EA-JU (It Must Happen) program. This program has led to the establishment of three industrial parks, new community facility buildings in most of the districts of the reservation, and more than 40 other projects now underway. This program is designed to upgrade opportunities of earning a decent living for the reservation population.

"With a solid industrial base established to assure adequate employment in most of the communities, a concurrent effort was begun to prepare individual Indian families to secure and hold the jobs arising out of this development. For many families the working head of a home had had only seasonal and undependable farm labor jobs as a means of support.

"Because of this pattern of work, many individuals were not prepared to accept steady, industrial employment. Compounding the problem of work habits were many social and family problems which also interfered with utilization of employment now available.

"For the past 20 months the Gila River Tribal Work Experience Program (TWEP) has helped people prepare themselves for the transition from seasonal employment to year around employment. In cooperation with the Tribal Council, employable heads of households, many of whom were known to have a high incidence of social and financial problems, were placed in various jobs in their own communities and received general assistance. These training participants were all employable persons whose eligibility for assistance was primarily the lack of available employment for which they were suited.

"Each community council was told that it could use the men for community improvement projects. The majority worked on housing improvement or water and sanitation projects. There were Indian foremen for all of the community crews. Workers received weekly assistance and the work training experience was related to many of the factors, attitudes and conditions which they would be facing in regular eight to five, five day a week employment in private industry. Bureau of Indian Affairs social services staff provided supporting help which was focused on maintaining the man on the work experience job.

"In less than two years of operating the program, the tribal work experience participants helped build 117 new homes and rehabilitate 77 existing houses. Numerous new roofs were built on other houses. Work experience crews helped complete four Public Health Service water and sanitation projects.

"Through June 1, 1969 a total of 198 family heads have participated in the Tribal Work Experience Program. Currently there are 36 active participants. A majority of those remaining have moved on to improved jobs in private industry, Federal agencies, farming, and other job training programs.

"Evaluation of this program indicates a decided positive and constructive influence in the lives of well over half of the work experience participants. In terms of such activities as attendance, work performance, tribal arrest record, there has been measurable change which signifies these people are leading more satisfying and useful lives.

"There has been sufficient positive change in work habits and attitudes to justify a focus on TWEP as a service program. A specific series of services was established to help participants prepare themselves for private employment. As participants show positive performance on the job they are given opportunity for more responsibility and self-management.

"A coordinating group was established which brought to bear many of the services available on the reservation directed toward preparing men for employment. These services included casework, social, and work experience evaluation, medical screening, aptitude testing, and prevocational adult education. Added to these services were two other factors which were essential to the job preparation program. One was to secure

Fig. 9.3   Pima and Maricopa women employed as key punch operators in a business in which the tribe has controlling interest.

a job pledge on which the trainee could depend. The other factor was confidence in the participant's ability to make the decisions which affected his own life and that of his family. As a result of the employment preparation services and improved work habits, 33 of the work experience participants have been placed in regular, private industrial jobs. An additional 20 participants were accepted for the Department of Labor's Mainstream program which is also geared towards moving its participants into employment as the individual is ready.

"Of the remaining 109 participants who have left the program, the greatest majority of these have found their own work without direct placement services as described above. An example of this: Six men were accepted by the Public Health Service based on their job performance while working on a community water project.

"A total experience of operating a tribal work experience program for the chronically unemployed, uneducated, and unskilled family head has been positive and constructive. The experience of the Gila River Community shows that with a beginning work-training placement geared to the ability of the participant, together with an adequate job arising out of the industrial development of the reservation, a person, regardless of background, education, and previous negative patterns of employment, can be successfully employed and thus provide an improved life for his family."[12]

10. Indian Education

Frank Lobo, Barry Bainton, and Thomas Weaver

Historical Perspective

FEDERAL RESPONSIBILITY for Indian education dates back to the earliest period of the Republic. This responsibility was first assumed by the U. S. government through treaty relationships established with tribes of the eastern seaboard. Treaties concluded with the Oneida, Tuscarora, and Stockbridge Indians on December 2, 1794, set a precedence which included provisions to provide educational facilities for these tribes. This procedure was to exert a strong influence on all future treaties concluded with American Indian tribes.

Prior to the early 1920s the basic philosophy underlying Indian education was aimed specifically at the total assimilation of the American Indian. The function of education in the assimilation process was seen as a logical conclusion by administrators. When the goal was not achieved, new strategies were developed in the field of education only to meet further resistance from the very people they were designed to change.

The basic assumption underlying federal Indian education policy is understandable when seen in the context of the developing national image held by European-Americans. The basis of this image was the "melting pot theory." Implicit in this theory is the idea that immigrants moving to the United States were expected to give up their customary ways of life before they could become "Americans."[1] Not only was this implicit understanding accepted by the newer arrivals, but it was internalized and accepted by them as one criteria of "Americanization." Paradoxically, it was assumed that American Indians would also follow this rite of passage and enter the mainstream of national life. Invariably, the assumption was that everyone would want to share in the opportunities offered by a developing industrial civilization. It never occurred to European-Americans that Indians did not want to change their culture, let alone voluntarily join the larger group.

Not until the mid 1920s did policy makers and educators perceive that this philosophy was due for a drastic overhaul. In 1926 the first major study of the entire federal-Indian relationship was undertaken at the request of the Department of the Interior with Lewis Meriam as director. The study entitled "The Problems of Indian Administration" was completed in 1928 and subsequently became known as the Meriam Report. Appealing for a revolutionary change in Indian administration, the report in essence called for the termination of government paternalism and an accelerated program to train Indians to administer their own affairs on the reservations. These recommendations were initially implemented in 1934 by the new commissioner of Indian affairs, John Collier.

By the turn of the century, three systems developed within the state of Arizona for the education of Indian children — the mission, federal, and public school systems. During the last quarter of the 1800s federal and mission schools formed a close working relationship, with the federal government providing financial assistance to the missionary schools. It was not until the close of the 1920s that the public schools system began to enroll Indian students in significant numbers. The basic shift from mis-

Fig. 10.1   A Navajo student diligently pursues her assignment at the Window Rock elementary school.

sion and federal to public schools continues today and with regard to their schools has become the policy of the federal government.

Mission Schools

In 1866, the Catholic archdiocese of Santa Fe attempted to open a mission school at San Xavier del Bac, Arizona. The project proved abortive and the school was moved to Tucson.

During the same time period, the U. S. government was encouraging missionary activity in the effort to Christianize the tribes allocated reservations throughout the country. Christianization dovetailed with the policy of the assimilation encouraged by government policy of the last half of the nineteenth century. Missionaries were believed to be dedicated and willing to endure isolation, privation, and low remuneration under circumstances which would discourage the lay teacher. Consequently, missionary efforts to establish schools in tribal areas received financial support from the federal government as early as the 1870s. In 1873 the first mission school in Arizona to receive support from the federal government was at San Xavier, ten miles south of Tucson. R. A. Wilbur, Papago agent, reported to the Indian commissioner:

I have received $2500.00 to be devoted to education purposes and with this sum I have erected a school house. The building is over one hundred feet long, surrounded by a good wall, and is conveniently divided into rooms for the accommodation of classes and teachers . . . .[2]

Missionaries were also hired by the Bureau of Indian Affairs to provide instruction to Indians. For example, Presbyterian missionaries were employed to teach in the Hopi area. Miss Charity Gaston, a Presbyterian, was assigned as instructor to the Navajos. Her counterpart, the Reverend C. H. Cook, taught the Pimas and Maricopas. The Dutch Reformed Church also had its representative at the San Tan Day School in the Pima Reservation in 1873.[3]

As recently as 1906, missionaries were also invited, at the discretion of individual directors, to provide compulsory religious instruction in federal schools.[4] In the 1890s missionaries participated in Indian education in 'contract schools." The contract school's physical plant was built and supported by the federal government, which also provided $31.25 per pupil and decided which courses would be taught. This type of school was operated in Tucson by the Presbyterians from 1888 to 1894.[5] Contract schools were operated through agreement with the Bureau of Indian Affairs until 1897, when public sentiment was aroused against the support of religious organizations with public monies. In 1897 Congress voted to curtail "appropriation for education in any sectarian school."[6] However, the inter-relationships between public and sectarian education were so complex that Congress continued to finance aspects of sectarian education from 1897 to 1900. In 1917, once again the policy for the separation of church and state was reaffirmed.[7]

From 1900 to 1925, missionary activity flourished in Arizona. The northern Navajo area was under the influence of the Presbyterians; the Apache area was under the control of the Lutherans, and the southernmost portion was under the jurisdiction of the Catholics. After the early 1920s missionary schools had a declining influence in Indian education. The shortage of operating funds both from their lay supporters and the federal government have been factors in the decline of mission schools. Other factors such as a vigorous building program of public schools off the reservations and federally-operated schools both on and off the reservations have greatly undercut the influence of the mission school in Indian education. In the same vein, the Meriam Report of 1928 lauded the pioneer efforts of the mission schools in many areas of Indian education, and at the same time, criticized the compulsory attendance on the part of federal school students at evangelistic meetings.[8] In 1934 John Collier, the acting commissioner of Indian affairs, issued a circular prohibiting compulsory attendance at religious services.

Federal Schools

In 1884 the agent of the Gila River Pimas suggested the construction of day schools for sedentary village dwellers. Intensive day school construction was initiated during the late 1890s among the tribes in northern Arizona.[9] By the turn of the century a similar program was in effect among the tribes in the southern portion of the state. Shortly after 1910, the Indian Service, once again, brought the needs of both the Navajos in the north and the Papagos in the south to the attention of Congress. But it was not until 1914, that Congress voted to establish more day and industrial schools, allocating $100,000.00 to the Navajos and some $50,000.00 to the Papagos.[10]

Despite increasing Congressional interest in the educational needs of the Indians of Arizona, the practical aspects of constructing schools in out-of-the-way locations defeated the best efforts. Schools among the two largest tribes in Arizona lagged behind expectations despite the emphasis of the new construction program. The sheer physical size and isolation of both the Papago and Navajo reservations was a major contributing factor. The complete lack of roads in some sectors and the broken nature of the country were other major obstacles to be dealt with before day schools could be established. Also mitigating against the day school was the economic way of life coupled with the social structure of the tribes involved. The sparse resources in both areas led to the development of a pastoral way of life. Of necessity, families developed widely separated low-density settlement patterns to avail themselves of natural forage for their livestock. Day schools were impractical in such an environment and these tribes continued to send their children to boarding schools both on and off the reservation.

From 1934 to 1944 the policy of the BIA was to phase itself out of the educational field. Nationally, 60 percent of the federal school system has been turned over to public schools. In Arizona, the same trend exists to phase out federal educational facilities and turn over the responsibility to the state and local governments. The statistics for state and local control of education in Arizona show 60 percent of Indian education is in federal hands with the remaining 40 percent the responsibility of public and other types of schools.[11]

Public Schools

Local public schools have also been utilized for the education of Indian children. Authorization to send Indian children residing on tax exempt land to public schools was promulgated by Commissioner T. J. Morgan in 1890, when he informed all state superintendents of public instruction that the BIA would make a payment of $10 per quarter per pupil to school districts.[12]

It was not until 1908 that Indians began taking advantage of the commissioner's authorization when six Pima children entered the public schools in Phoenix and Mesa, Arizona. In 1918 the number had increased to nineteen children in public schools. Sixteen were from the Colorado River Reservation, two from the Papago Reservation, and one from the Pima Reservation. By 1921, 182 Indian children had entered public school.[13] Public school attendance had risen slightly by 1925 to 195, or 2.4 percent of the total Indian student population of 8,080 who were attending federal and mission schools in Arizona. Since the implementation of the Indian Reorganization Act of 1934, the public school system has received a steadily accelerating number of students from reservations. Special legislation has encouraged the public school system to take on the responsibility of an increased Indian student enrollment without an undue cost to the tax base of local school systems.

Contemporary Indian Education

According to statistics released by the Interior Department in 1969, there were 45,139 school age Indian children between the ages of five and eighteen in the state.[14] Of this total, 40,430[15] were actually attending

Fig. 10.2   Children in a modern reservation school.

one of three types of educational institutions previously identified: schools financed by the federal government through the Bureau of Indian Affairs; public schools financed by state government; and a smaller number of mission schools supported by their societies.

Federal Schools

Three types of federal schools for Indian students are operated in the state of Arizona: the boarding school, the day school, and a combination of the two. In 1969, there were 17,010 Indian students enrolled in forty-eight boarding and day schools in Arizona.[16] This figure does not include the four dormitories which house students attending public schools located at Flagstaff, Holbrook, Snowflake, and Winslow. The greatest concentration of federal boarding schools is in the Window Rock area in Arizona. In 1969, twenty-nine federal schools were in operation within the Navajo Reservation. These included 12,266 students in eleven regular

TABLE 10.1

Federal Schools in Arizona, 1969

Type of School	No. of Schools	Boarding Enrollment	Day Enrollment	Total
Window Rock Area				
Boarding	11	5,535		5,535
Boarding and Day	15	4,956	1,117	6,073
Day	3		658	658
Total (Window Rock)	29	10,491	1,775	12,226
Phoenix Area				
Boarding	3	1,573		1,573
Boarding and day	1	81	1,124	1,205
Day	15		1,966	1,966
Total (Phoenix)	19	1,654	3,090	4,744
TOTAL	48	12,145	4,865	17,010

Source: Drawn from, *Statistics Concerning Indian Education,* Office of Education, Bureau of Indian Affairs, U.S. Department of the Interior, Haskell Institute, Lawrence, Kansas, 1969, tables 4 and 5. These statistics are based on the annual attendance reports of schools operated by the Bureau of Indian Affairs and cover all students enrolled regardless of age.

boarding schools, fifteen combined boarding and day schools, and three regular day schools. The combined boarding and day school allocates a portion of its facilities for a day school for pupils located in the immediate vicinity of the boarding school.

A parallel group of boarding and boarding/day schools is maintained by the Phoenix area office. Unlike the Navajo Reservation with its high population concentration, the eighteen reservations under the control of the Phoenix area office are dispersed throughout the state. There are three boarding schools and one combined boarding and day school with a total of 1,654 pupils at Keams Canyon, Phoenix, Fort Apache, and Santa Rosa. In addition, fifteen day schools serve 1,966 students at the Truxton Canyon, Fort Apache, Hopi, Papago, Pima, and Salt River reservations.

Table 10.1 summarizes the federal school enrollment in Arizona.

The federal school system maintains only one secondary school in Arizona, the Phoenix Indian School in Phoenix. In order to avoid building costly primary and secondary schools the federal government has constructed peripheral dormitories on Indian or federal land and sends the students boarded there to public schools near these peripheral dormitories. This is consistent with BIA policy of withdrawing from education and turning the function over to the public school systems of the various states.[17] The cost of the education of these students is shared by the state and federal governments under Johnson-O'Malley funds. At present there are 1,120 Indian students in Arizona receiving education under this provision in northern Arizona at Flagstaff, Holbrook, Winslow, and Snowflake. The program combines the advantages of the day school with that of the boarding school. An atmosphere more congenial to learning prevails in that the pupils are able to perfect their language skills and broaden their view of the area outside the reservation by direct contact during the school day.

Public Schools

Public schools are playing an increasingly active part in the education of Indian children. In addition to the 17,230 Indian students enrolled in federally-sponsored schools, there are 18,686 pupils attending Arizona public schools.[18] The Indian student in Arizona is faced with one or more of the following circumstances with regard to the public school system. The public school district may lie completely outside the reservation boundaries; it may overlap a part or all of the reservation, such as the Blackwater School on the Gila River Reservation which is a part of Coolidge School District Number 21; or it may fall completely within the reservation, such as Indian Oasis School District Number 40 on the Papago Reservation. The particular location of the school districts relative to trust lands raises certain problems which will be discussed below.

Off the reservations, state and local governments provide educational services based on tax assessment. Public school districts may overlap and sometimes completely surround reservations, but the local districts cannot tax federal land held in trust by the federal government which lies within their own districts. Indian children residing on these federal lands were previously considered ineligible to attend public school. State and local authorities maintained that school districts would be incurring a financial overburden if Indian children were educated through the state's budget. Since 1934 the federal government has provided funding to states and local school districts to make up the deficits resulting from the education of Indian children who live on tax-exempt land.

In 1969-70 there were 13,922 students in the public schools whose costs were covered by the Johnson-O'Malley funding under Public Law 73-167. These funds totalled $4,510,000.00, an increase of $381,871.00

TABLE 10.2

Districts and Expenditures of Johnson-O'Malley Participating Schools, 1969-1970

County	Number of Participating School Districts	Expenditures of Johnson-O'Malley Funds	Number of Indian Students
Apache	6	$1,478,039.72	5,622
Coconino	4	552,502.56	1,553
Gila	2	248,791.97	1,078
Graham	2	113,324.77	356
Maricopa	8	59,459.75	774
Mohave	4	5,988.67	160
Navajo	6	1,704,347.28	2,176
Pima	1	81,913.90	772
Pinal	7	166,046.09	914
Yuma	4	25,386.06	517
TOTAL		$4,435,800.77	13,922
ADMINISTRATION		74,206.51	
TOTAL		$4,510,007.28	

Source: E. L. Turner, Jr., *et al., Annual Report, The Division of Indian Education of the Arizona State Department of Public Instruction to the Bureau of Indian Affairs, 1969-1970,* Phoenix.

from 1968-69.[19] In essence, the Johnson-O'Malley Act is federal recognition of its financial obligation to local governments on one hand and the federal responsibility to provide services to Indians in federal trust lands on the other.

In order for a state to qualify for Johnson-O'Malley funds it must negotiate a contract with the federal government establishing terms under which aid is granted. The contract with the federal government is voluntary by both parties, and both are free to renegotiate the contract at the expiration date set in the agreement. Arizona has renegotiated its Johnson-O'Malley contract numerous times in response to new conditions since the late 1930s. The expenditure of Johnson-O'Malley funds for Arizona in 1969-70 is shown in Table 10.2.

Two other pieces of legislation that have proved vital in financing Indian education have been the Federal Impact Laws (Public Laws 81-874 and 81-815), and the Elementary and Secondary Education Act (Public Law 89-10). Both Public Laws 81-874 and 81-815 supplement the Johnson-O'Malley Act as a source of funds for Indian education.

TABLE 10.3

Summary of the Federal Impact Laws

County	P.L. 81-874	P.L. 81-815
Apache	$1,546,250.00	$1,202,021.26
Cochise	998,704.00	—0—
Coconino	850,035.00	30,654.43
Gila	207,089.00	18,216.30
Graham	98,032.00	—0—
Maricopa	1,685,913.00	693,492.77
Mohave	60,810.00	—0—
Navajo	828,822.00	175,448.49
Pima	2,128,467.00	848,177.00
Pinal	316,188.00	—0—
Santa Cruz	34,543.00	—0—
Yavapai	89,967.00	—0—
Yuma	653,906.00	—0—
TOTAL	$9,498,726.00	$2,968,010.25

Source: W. P. Shofstall, *et al., Annual Report of the Superintendent of Public Instruction, 1969-1970,* p. 136–37; 312–13, Phoenix.

School districts who qualify for aid from the federal government for the education of Indian pupils must first apply for aid under either or both of the Federal Impact Laws. If a deficit still exists then Johnson-O'Malley funds fill the deficiency.

Congress had originally enacted the Federal Impact Laws to reimburse school districts in "lieu of taxes" resulting from federal activity, such as aiding school districts for the education of the children of military or defense personnel. Public Law 874 was designed to provide for the operation and maintenance costs of these schools. Public Law 815 was similar in intent, but contributed funds specifically for school expansion and construction.

In 1953, Public Law 815 was amended to authorize the construction of public schools who enrolled Indian students. It was not until 1958 that Public Law 874 was amended to supplement the Johnson-O'Malley Act of 1934 to provide monies in "lieu of taxes" to local school districts who enrolled Indian children in public schools. Table 10.3 shows the disbursement of Federal Impact monies to counties in Arizona under the Federal Impact Laws.

It is difficult to arrive at precise figures concerning the disbursement

TABLE 10.4

Head Start Programs in Arizona

Tribe	Number of Centers	Approx. No. of Children
Navajo	102	2000
Hopi	5	125
Colorado River	1	148
Gila River	8	255
Hualapai	1	56
Havasupai	1	25
Papago	6	120
Salt River	3	45
San Carlos	2	100
Whiteriver	10	150
Yavapai	1	20
TOTAL	140	3044

Source: M. Bogan, Arizona State University, "Indian Head Start Program in Arizona, 1970," mimeo report.

of funds to the Indian community from Public Law 847 and 815. Johnson-O'Malley funding is made from the Department of the Interior through the superintendent of public instruction to the local level, specifically earmarked for Indians. In the case of Public Law 874 and 815, funding is made directly from the Department of Health, Education, and Welfare to the local school districts and federal schools for the benefit of aiding in the education of Indians, non-Indian ethnic groups and military and federal personnel.

In addition to the specially funded educational arrangements discussed above are the Head Start Programs funded through the Office of Economic Opportunity. Table 10.4 lists the number of Indian pupils in schools present in Arizona.

Mission and Other Schools

A total of 3,393 Arizona Indian students were enrolled in non-federal and non-public schools in 1969.[20] The majority of these students attended mission or religious-sponsored schools. Private schools contribute little statistically to the total educational picture of Indian students

Fig. 10.3   The Pisinemo Brass and String Ensemble at
San José Mission, Papago Reservation.

in primary and secondary grades. In recent years the role of the mission
school has declined under the competition from the federal and public
systems, and from the shortage of operating funds. In southern Arizona
on the Papago Reservation, for example, mission school facilities have
closed or been turned over to the public school system. Despite the declining importance of church-related schools, they are still an alternative to the
federal and public secondary schools in some local circumstances.

Problems in Indian Education

The serious problems inherent in Indian education were first brought
to public attention by the massive Meriam Report, the recommendations
of which were implemented by John Collier, the commissioner of Indian
affairs, in 1934. During Collier's administration, Indians were encouraged
to achieve greater independence in the management of their own affairs.

However, the programs initiated by John Collier were greatly curtailed by the advent of the Second World War. From the Second World War to the mid 1960s, the conduct of Indian affairs has been subjected to the philosophy of the administration in office on one hand, and to the priorities of Congress on the other.

By the 1960s, the social sciences had sufficiently developed their methodologies to initiate studies of the position of minority groups within the larger society. Social dislocations and antagonisms often culminating in social eruptions in urban and ghetto life have given a sense of urgency to both social scientists and the general public to find solutions to these problems. It was in keeping with the above trends that Congress, in August, 1967, ordered a study of the relationships of Indians to the larger society. Attention was primarily focused on two aspects of Indian life: health and education, with the emphasis given to the latter. The examination of Indian education culminated in the massive seven volume hearings before the U.S. Senate Subcommittee on Indian Education in 1967-69.[21] The hearings point to problems plaguing Indian education today and suggest solutions.

The Senate Subcommittee Hearings

The initial resolution creating the special subcommittee stated that it was to examine, investigate, and make a complete study of any and all matters pertaining to the education and related problems of Indian children. The subcommittee was chaired by the late Robert F. Kennedy and staffed by Wayne Morse, Oregon; Harrison A. Williams, Jr., New Jersey; Ralph Yarborough, Texas; Paul J. Fannin, Arizona; and Peter H. Dominick, Colorado. In order to sensitize themselves to the special conditions existing on the local level, the subcommittee conducted hearings in the following locations; Fairbanks, Alaska; Portland, Oregon; Pine Ridge, South Dakota; Flagstaff, Arizona; and Twin Oaks, Oklahoma; as well as in Washington, D.C. The resulting study points a dark picture of the nation's negligence in its responsibilities to the educational needs of Indian youth.

A summary of the subcommittee's findings on the state of Indian education on a national level follows:

1. Dropout rates are twice the national average.
2. The level of formal education is half the national average.
3. Achievement levels are far below those of their non-Indian counterparts.
4. The Indian child falls progessively behind the longer he stays in school.

Even though nine out of ten Indian children are in school the question remains: why has the educational system failed in the education of Indian youth? The reasons are myriad, but they can be divided into two broad categories.

First, there are those problems that impinge on the Indian from outside his immediate world. These include such problems as the relationship of the Indian relative to the state and federal government, and the political and economic aspects of the non-Indian society. The second broad category of problems are intrinsic to the social structure and culture of Indians, such as custom, language, and self-evaluation.

The committee examined the most important factors contributing to the problems of Indian education — the social-economic disadvantage of the Indian family. They found that:

1. The average Indian's annual income is $1,500 — 75 percent below the national average.
2. The unemployment rate is ten times the national average.
3. The average Indian lives ten years less than the average non-Indian.
4. The death rate for Indian children is twice as high as the national average.[22]

Table 10.5 presents the educational and familial factors which influence poor achievement among Indian children.

Indian Academic Performance

One of the many exhibits submitted to the subcommittee was a

TABLE 10.5
Social-Economic Factors Comparing
Indians to the General U.S. Population

	Indians	General U.S. Population
Median family income	$1,500	$6,882
Unemployment rate	45%	4.6%
Average life expectancy	63.5 years	70.2 years
Infant mortality rate (per 1,000 live births)	35.9	24.8
Average schooling for adults	5 years	11.7 years
Average school dropout rate	50%	29.0%

Source: U.S., Senate, Subcommittee on Education, 90th Cong., 1969, pt. 1:130.

study of the academic performances of the Indians of the Southwest. The study focused on a six-state area, Arizona, Nevada, New Mexico, Oklahoma, southern Colorado, and southern Utah, having as its objective the examination of the high school dropout problem. The researchers found that:

The dropout rates for male and female students are almost identical, the percentage for males being 38.6 and that for females 38.7 percent. It should be noted that the total dropout rate of 38.7 percent includes grades eight through twelve. Many studies base high school dropout rates upon enrollment of students in grades nine through twelve. In this study, the dropout rate from grade nine to grade twelve inclusive is 30.6 precent.[23]

Within Arizona five tribal areas were sampled. Dropout rates ranged from a high of 60 percent to a low of 15 percent with an average rate of 37 percent. The authors expressed deep concern over the eighth grade dropout rate. They stated that few of these will have the opportunity to develop marketable skills and realize the full potential of their inherent talents.[24]

A parallel study by William H. Kelly, covering the southern portion of the state of Arizona, examined both the dropout and achievement rates of school age children, one-quarter or more Indian blood, residing on reservations. Kelly concluded that:

1. The high school dropout rate is serious, with 22.3 percent of all Indian students between the ages of sixteen and eighteen leaving school before graduation. Most seriously affected are the girls with a rate of 24.5 percent.
2. The unexpected finding is that Indian students, once they enter high school, go through to graduation with little trouble provided they stay in school. The retention (held back) rate is less than for non-Indians (2.6% compared with 3.8%).
3. A substantial majority of Indian students are behind in grade as measured by age. Many Indian mothers do not send their children to school until they are seven, and a high percentage of Indian children spend four years getting through the first three grades.
4. Among Indian students in the first three grades, those who attend federal day schools are much more apt to be retained in grade than those who attend public schools.[25]

An unexpected finding of Kelly's study was the discovery that many youths in the age bracket sixteen to eighteen were either unaccounted for or completely unknown to the local school authorities. Kelly states the following in his conclusions to the study:

We found not just a few but a whopping 340 in the sixteen through eighteen age category alone . . . . An estimated additional 894 in the six through fifteen age group remain unknown and unaccounted for in our statistics.[26]

Kelly concluded that before Indian education can be improved, schools and educational agencies must conduct and maintain records adequate to build a base from which the improvement of Indian education may be launched.

Two indices of low achievement of Indian students stand out. First, the dropout rate among Indian students is very high. Of those who enter first grade, approximately 25 percent graduate from high school, which means that there is a 75 percent dropout rate between the first grade and high school graduation.[27] This dropout rate, of course, varies from tribe to tribe. However, among Indian students in Arizona the dropout rate is consistently much higher than that of comparable non-Indian students. More importantly, the dropout rate is indicative of the educational disadvantage which many Arizona citizens of Indian background have in competing economically with non-Indians.

Another index of low achievement is that the majority of Indian students are behind in their grade level as measured by standard age for any given grade. This is either due to late entrance into school or to retention in any grade for more than one year. An estimated 86 percent of Indian students in the sixteen to eighteen age range are behind in their expected grade level for their age.[28]

Cultural Problems

Why do Indian students show such low achievement ratings? A major factor is the set of problems created by cross-cultural communication which add further complexities to the already intricate interplay between the educational institution and the Indian student. By the time the Indian child enters school, he has been enculturated into the way of life of his tribe and is a functioning member of his society. This enculturation process includes among other things: language, training in bodily movements and handling of objects, training in the accepted manner in which to relate to relatives and other individuals with whom the child has close contact, training in values, and world view.

The Indian child, much like his non-Indian counterpart, enters school as an enculturated individual reflecting viewpoints of his cultural group. The substance and the manner in which the Indian child has been enculturated is often radically different from that of the non-Indian. The Indian child very often enters what is to him a foreign educational institution. Not only does the Indian child often lack the home training which most non-Indians receive, and which the school assumes he has received, but often the Indian child's training in his tribal culture creates dissonance in the non-Indian world. For example, in some Indian tribes, a child may be punished at home for aggressive behavior, while at school, he is expected to be self-assertive and aggressively competitive. Competition itself is a predominating value in the non-Indian culture, but it is not similarly valued by many Indians. A teacher notes:

When I taught school in Phoenix I successfully used gold stars as a way to motivate the students. By that, I mean I would give a gold star for a perfect paper and I had a chart on the wall with every child's name. The children all worked very hard to earn one of the gold stars. Now I'm teaching Indian students and I tried my gold stars. At first I couldn't understand why an Indian child never got more than one gold star. It seemed as if they would deliberately miss so as not to receive a gold star. Finally one of the Indian employees told me that these children don't like to be singled out from the rest of the group as being better . . . . In other words, the teaching techniques that worked for me in Phoenix did not work for me on this Indian reservation.[29]

The language problem experienced by many students is only one of the more obvious of the many clashes between Indian and non-Indian culture. As pointed out by the linguist Edward Sapir, each language embodies the conceptual categories of the speakers of the language. These conceptual categories are means of expressing a native speaker's cognitive conceptualization of his entire universe. Kluckhohn and Leighton have pointed out that:

The forms of each language impose upon its speakers certain positive predispositions and certain negative restrictions as to the meanings they find in their experience.[30]

Navajo speakers for example, have many complex descriptive terms which are lacking in English. The complexity of the Navajo language is demonstrated in the following examples:

. . . where in English one word "rough" (more pedantically, "rough-surfaced") may equally well be used to describe a road, a rock, and the business surface of a file, Navaho finds a need for three different words which may not be used interchangeably. While the general tendency is for Navaho to make finer and more concrete distinctions, this is not invariably the case. The same stem is used for "rip," "light beam," and "echo," ideas which seem diverse to white people.[31]

Whorf has written that the Hopi conceptualization of the passage of time as expressed in their language differs considerably from that of English speakers.[32] Therefore, learning a new language, particularly one as unrelated as English, is not simply learning a new vocabulary, but involves entirely new sets of cognitive categories and conceptualizations of such things as man and his relationship to time, space, and movement.

A concerted effort has been made in Arizona since 1965, to aid Indian children in the linguistic problems mentioned above. Under the Elementary and Secondary Act (Public Law 89-10), funds were made available to the local districts to implement special programs, such as learning English as a second language. The goal of the program is to teach English to four and five year old children in preparation for regular course work in the primary grades. These classes are designated as "beginners" classes and are distinguished from regular kindergarten classes in that they teach English as a second language. The classes are taught primarily in the native language, which is then gradually replaced in kindergarten and first grade with instruction in English.

Edward Hall has written of the importance of the "silent language" which all persons utilize in communicating through body movement. By the time the Indian child enters school, he has learned the motor habits acceptable to his tribe. At home, the Indian child may be taught to avoid prolonged eye contact as indicative of aggressive behavior. At school, the child who looks at his desk and not at the teacher may have this behavior construed as being impolite or inattentive. In fact he may be giving his teacher his full attention.

Obviously, many of the values held by various tribes are not congruent with those of non-Indian society. The Indian child entering school must not only learn the subject matter being taught, but often a new language and value orientation as well. The teacher is not always aware of the extent to which an Indian child entering school has learned a cultural system which is markedly different from the non-Indian one on which the educational institution is based. Teachers in Arizona are not required to take courses in Indian culture, in cultural differences, or in cross-cultural communication. In addition, only twenty-five teachers in Arizona are themselves Indian.[33]

Adequate teaching is based on adequate communication. Even if both the Indian student and teacher are speaking the same language, communication is a complex procedure. Teachers without an awareness of Indian culture are not effective communicators; Indian students who have received their enculturation in a tribal and not in the non-Indian culture are poor receivers of this communication.

Very few Indian parents have an opportunity to influence the manner in which their children are educated. The educational institutions in Arizona are administered primarily by non-Indians, and are aimed at educating non-Indians. Much of the material and the manner in which it is presented is seen as irrelevant to the life goals of the Indian student and his parents. Rough Rock Demonstration School on the Navajo Reservation is one of the few exceptions to this generalization. Rough Rock has an all-Indian board of directors. The students are taught not only the usual curriculum, but also much of the traditional Navajo knowledge. Indian teachers, as well as the Navajo language, are utilized whenever possible. The public school at Blackwater on the Gila River Reservation also has an Indian school board which functions in the same manner as a school board outside of a reservation. Mention should also be made of the Navajo Community College which receives support from the Navajo Nation and is controlled by a Navajo board of regents with a Navajo president.

Both Indians and non-Indians have a vested interest in education and recognize it as a means for the betterment of the quality of life in both communities. What is equally apparent is that the methods used in the instruction of non-Indians are not properly adjusted to communicate this academic process across a cultural hiatus to the Indian community. If education is to have relevance to the needs and desires of the Indians' community, emphasis must be placed on bridging the cultural gulf between diverse ethnic communities. Arizona's future prosperity will depend upon an educated and skilled citizenry who are able to provide themselves with a measure of self-sufficiency and personal fulfillment. An educational process that is adjusted to their culture will aid in achieving this goal.

Notes to the Chapters

Pages 41 – 77

3. HISTORICAL FOUNDATIONS

1. Theodore H. Hass, "The Legal Aspects of Indian Affairs From 1887 To 1957," *The Annals of the American Academy of Political and Social Science,* May, 1957, p. 16.

4. THE TWENTIETH CENTURY

1. William H. Kelly, *Indian Affairs and the Indian Reorganization Act: The Twenty Year Record* (Tucson: The University of Arizona, 1954), p. 3.
2. D'Arcy McNickle, *The Indian Tribes of the United States* (London and New York: Oxford University Press, 1962), pp. 56-57.
3. James E. Officer, *Indians in School* (Tucson: Bureau of Ethnic Research, The University of Arizona, 1956), p. 36.
4. William Zimmerman, Jr., "The Role of the Bureau of Indian Affairs Since 1933," *The Annals of the American Academy of Political and Social Science,* May, 1957, p. 32.
5. Kelly, *op. cit.,* p. 6.
6. *Ibid.,* p. 26.
7. *Ibid.,* p. 4.
8. Zimmerman, *op. cit.,* p. 34.
9. *Ibid.,* p. 35.
10. *Ibid.*
11. Arthur V. Watkins, "Termination of Federal Supervision: Disintegration and the American Indians," *The Annals of the American Academy of Political and Social Science,* May, 1957, p. 50.
12. *Ibid.,* p. 51.
13. Murray L. Crosse, "Criminal and Civil Jurisdiction in Indian Country," *Arizona Law Review,* vol. 4, no. 1, 1962, p. 61.

5. CONTEMPORARY ARIZONA INDIANS

1. Officer, *Indians in School,* p. 2.
2. Nancy O. Lurie, "The Indian Claims Commission Act," *The Annals of the American Academy of Political and Social Science,* May, 1957, p. 62.

6. THE URBAN INDIAN: MAN OF TWO WORLDS

1. U.S., Department of Commerce, Bureau of the Census, *Census of the Population: 1970, General Social and Economic Characteristics, Final Report PC (1) C4, Arizona,* 1971.
2. Edward H. Spicer, *Cycles of Conquest: The Impact of Spain, Mexico and the United States on the Indians of the Southwest, 1533-1960.* (Tucson, The University of Arizona Press, 1962), p. 468; Shichi Nagata, "The Reservation Community and the Urban Community: Hopi Indians of Moencopi," in *The American Indian in Urban Society,* ed. Jack O. Waddell and O. Michael Watson (Boston: Little, Brown and Company, 1971), pp. 115-159.

3. Roger E. Kelly and John O. Cramer, *American Indians in Small Cities: A Survey of Urban Acculturation in Two Northern Arizona Communities,* Rehabilitation Monographs no. 1. (Flagstaff: Northern Arizona University, 1966).

4. Kelly and Cramer, *op. cit.,; Nagata, op. cit.,; Theodore E. Graves, "Alternative Models for the Study of Urban Migration," *Human Organization,* vol. 25, no. 4, 1966, p. 296; Wesley R. Hurt, Jr., "The Urbanization of the Yankton Indians," *Human Organization,* vol. 20, no. 4, 1961-1962, p. 226-231; James Hirabagashi et al., "Urban Indian Integration: Final Report," unpublished manuscript (San Francisco State, 1964).

5. Nagata, *op. cit.,* p. 116.

6. Kelly and Cramer, *op. cit.*

7. William H. Kelly, Statement at Arizona Commission of Indian Affairs Meeting, 1958, unpublished manuscript, Tucson, Bureau of Ethnic Research, The University of Arizona.

8. *Tucson Daily Citizen,* February 26, 1971, p. 31.

9. Arizona State Employment Service, *Manpower Services to Arizona Indians, 1969,* (Phoenix, June 1970), p. 11. Hereafter sited as ASES.

10. Benjamin J. Taylor and Dennis J. O'Connor, *Indian Manpower Resources in the Southwest: A Pilot Study,* (Tempe: Bureau of Business and Economic Research, Arizona State University, 1969).

11. ASES, *op. cit.,* p. 13.

12. Taylor and O'Connor, *op. cit.,* p. 359.

13. ASES, *op. cit.,* p. 16.

14. ASES, *Ibid.,* p. 19.

15. Judge Magnum, "The Urban Indian: An Overview Study," mimeographed. (Phoenix, Arizona, 1968), p. 14.

16. Carroll Barber, "Trilingualism in Pascua: The Social Functions of Language in an Arizona Yaqui Village." (Master's thesis, The University of Arizona, 1952), in Fernando Escalante, "A Compendium of Excessive Drinking and Alcoholism Among Yaqui Indians in Old Pascua Village," mimeographed. (Tucson: The University of Arizona, 1971).

17. U.S., Congress, Senate, Subcommittee on Indian Education, *Indian Education: A National Tragedy — A National Challenge,* 1969, p. 17-19.

18. William H. Kelly, *A Study of Southern Arizona School-age Indian Children, 1966-1967.* (Tucson: Bureau of Ethnic Research, The University of Arizona, 1967).

19. Willard P. Bass, *The American Indian High School Graduate* (Albuquerque: Southwestern Cooperative Educational Laboratory, Inc., 1969).

20. *Ibid.,* p. 38.

21. *Ibid.*

7. THE LEGAL BASIS OF TRIBAL GOVERNMENT

1. Wall v. Williamson, 8 Ala. 48, 51, 1854.

2. Worcester v. Georgia, 6 Pet. 515, 1832.

3. 16 Stat. 544, 566, 25 U.S.C. 71.

4. Arenas v. United States, 60 F Supp. VII, 1945.

5. 8 Wheat. 543, 1823.

6. Worcester v. Georgia, 6 Pet. 515, 1832.

7. 60 Stat. 1950.

8. H. Rept. No. 474, Comm. Ind. Aff., 23rd Cong., 1st sess., May 20, 1834.

9. 118 U.S. 375, 1886.

10. Worcester v. Georgia, *supra.*

11. 1 Op. A.G. 645, 1824.

12. Prentice and Egan, *The Commerce Clause of the Federal Constitution,* 1898.

13. 266 U.S., 481, 1925.

14. United States v. Hellard, 322 U.S. 363, 1944.
15. Monroe Price, "Law and Social Order," *Arizona State Law Journal,* vol. 2, 1969, p. 161.
16. Act of July 9, 1832, 4 Stat. 564, 25 U.S.C. 1-2.
17. 9 Stat. 395, 5 U.S.C. 485.
18. 42 L.D. 493, 499, 1913.
19. United States v. Arenas, 158, F. 2d, 730, 747, 1947.
20. F. S. Cohen, "Indians are Citizens," *The American Indian,* 1944.
21. 67 Stat. 588, 18 U.S.C. 1162, 1360.
22. 358 U.S. 217, 1959.
23. Warren Trading Post v. Tax Commission, 380 U.S. 685, 1965.
24. 55 I.D. 15, 1934.
25. *Ibid.*

8. LIVING CONDITIONS

1. Indian Health Service, Phoenix Area Office, PHS Form 2500, *Indian Premise and Home Environmental Health Survey Data,* 1970.
2. Bureau of Indian Affairs, Phoenix Area Office, *Indian Housing,* 1970.
3. *Op. cit.* PHS Form 2500.
4. *Op. cit.* Indian Housing.
5. *Ibid.*
6. Navajo Area Indian Health Service, Health Programs, Health Program Deficiencies, and Justification for Increased FY 1971 Resources, prepared at request of the Navajo tribe, 1970.
7. *Ibid.*
8. Arizona Commission of Indian Affairs, *Phoenix Annual Report,* 1970.
9. *Op. cit.,* Navajo Area Indian Health Service.

9. EMPLOYMENT, ECONOMIC DEVELOPMENT AND ASSISTANCE PROGRAMS

1. Arizona State Employment Service, *Manpower Services to Arizona Indians, 1969,* June 1970, Phoenix.
2. Bureau of Indian Affairs, Phoenix, *Information Profiles of Indian Reservations in Arizona, Nevada, Utah,* July, 1970.
3. *Op. cit.,* Manpower Services, 1970.
4. *Ibid.*
5. *Ibid.*
6. *Ibid.*
7. Arizona Commission of Indian Affairs, Annual Report, 1970, Phoenix.
8. *Ibid.*
9. *Ibid.*
10. Bureau of Indian Affairs, Social Service Program, 1969, a statement from the Bureau of Social Services, Washington, D.C.
11. Letter dated November 25, 1970, from M. L. Schwartz, Assistant Area Director, Bureau of Indian Affairs, Phoenix Area Office.
12. Bureau of Indian Affairs, Indian Record, August 1969, a report from the Office of Indian Commissioner, Washington, D.C.

10. INDIAN EDUCATION IN ARIZONA

1. J. B. Salpointe, *Soldiers of the Cross,* Banning, California, 1898, pp. 251-252, St. Boniface's Industrial School, quoted in James E. Officer, *Indians in School,* Tucson, Bureau of Ethnic Research, University of Arizona, 1956, p. 8.
2. U.S., Department of the Interior, *Report of the Commissioner of Indian Affairs,* 1873, p. 284, quoted in James E. Officer, *Indians in School,* Tucson, Bureau of Ethnic Research, University of Arizona, 1956, p. 103.

3. Officer, *op. cit.,* p. 103.
4. *Ibid.*
5. *Ibid.,* p. 104.
6. *Illinois ex rel. McCullum v. Board of Education,* 333 U.S. 203, (1948), quoted in Department of the Interior, *Federal Indian Law,* New York City, New York: Association on American Indian Affairs, 1958, p. 119.
7. Act of March 2, 1917, 39 Stat. 969, 988, U.S.C. 278, quoted in Department of the Interior, *Federal Indian Law,* New York City, New York: Association on American Indian Affairs, 1958, p. 279.
8. Lewis Meriam, *et. al., The Problems of Indian Administration,* Baltimore, Maryland, 1928, p. 411, quoted in James E. Officer, *Indians in School,* Tucson, Bureau of Ethnic Research, University of Arizona, 1956, p. 110.
9. James E. Officer, *Indians in School,* Tucson, Bureau of Ethnic Research, University of Arizona, 1956, p. 12.
10. U.S., Department of the Interior, *Report of the Commissioner of Indian Affairs,* 1915, p. 5, quoted in James E. Officer, *Indians in School,* Tucson, Bureau of Ethnic Research, University of Arizona, 1956, p. 13.
11. Phoenix Area Office, Bureau of Indian Affairs, "Program Activities, 1969," mimeo report.
12. U.S., Department of the Interior, *Report of the Commissioner of Indian Affairs,* 1890, CLLXIX, quoted in James E. Officer, *Indians in School,* Tucson, Bureau of Ethnic Research, University 1956, p. 14.
13. James E. Officer, *Indians in School,* Tucson, Bureau of Ethnic Research, University of Arizona, 1956, p. 14.
14. U.S., Department of the Interior, *Statistics Concerning Indian Education,* Lawrence, Kansas, Haskell Institute, 1969, Table #1, p. 7. These statistics are based on the enumeration of all Indian children from 5 to 18 years.
15. In addition there are 3,090 students over 18 enumerated by the BIA which have not been included in the following statistical discussion. Data obtained from: U.S. Department of the Interior, 1969, *ibid.,* Table #1, p. 8.
16. *Ibid.,* Table #1, p. 9.
17. *Ibid.,* Table #1, p. 5.
18. *Ibid.,* Table #1, p. 9.
19. E. L. Turner, *et al, Annual Report, the Division of Indian Education of the Arizona State Department of Public Instruction to the Bureau of Indian Affairs, 1969-1970,* Phoenix, mimeographed report; W. P. Shofstall, *et al, Annual Report, Superintendent of Public Instruction,* 1968-1969, Phoenix, mimeographed report, p. 49.
20. U.S., Department of the Interior, *Statistics Concerning Indian Education,* Lawrence, Kansas, Haskell Institute, 1969, Table #1, p. 9.
21. U.S., Senate, *Hearings Before the Subcommittee on Indian Education,* 90th Congress, Washington, D.C., 1969.
22. *Ibid.* Part 1, p. 5.
23. Charles S. Owens and Willard P. Bass, *The American Indian High School Dropout in the Southwest,* (Albuquerque: Southwestern Cooperative Educational Laboratory, Inc., 1969), p. 7.
24. *Ibid.,* p. 8.
25. W. K. Kelly, "A Study of Southern Arizona School-Age Indian Children, 1966-1967," Tucson, Bureau of Ethnic Research, University of Arizona, 1967.
26. *Ibid.,* p. 36.
27. U.S., Senate, Subcommittee on Indian Education, 91st Congress, *Field Investigation and Research Reports,* 1969, vol. 2, p. 217.
28. Kelly, *ibid.*

29. Robert A. Roessell, Jr., "Indian Education in Arizona," *Journal of American Indian Education,* vol. 1, no. 1. (Tempe, Arizona State University, College of Education, June, 1961).

30. Clyde Kluckhohn and Dorothea Leighton, *The Navajo,* Garden City, Doubleday and Company, 1969, p. 182.

31. *Ibid.,* p. 277-278.

32. B. J. Whorf, "An American Indian Model of the Universe," pp. 57-64, quoted in J. B. Carroll, (ed.), *Language Thought and Reality,* New York: John Wiley and Sons, Inc., 1958.

33. Subcommittee on Indian Education, *Field Investigation and Research Reports, op. cit.,* p. 225.

Suggested Readings

CHAPTERS 3, 4, 5

Collier, John. *Indians of the Americas,* New York: W. W. Norton & Company, Inc., 1947.

Deloria, Vine, Jr. *Custer Died for Your Sins: An Indian Manifesto.* New York: The Macmillan Company, 1969.

Deloria, Vine, Jr. *We Talk, You Listen.* New York: The Macmillan Company, 1970.

Josephy, Alvin M., Jr. *The Indian Heritage of America.* New York: Alfred A. Knopf, 1968.

McNickle, D'Arcy. *Indian Tribes of the United States.* London & New York: Oxford University Press, 1962.

Simpson, George E., and J. Milton Yinger, ed. "American Indians and American Life," *The Annals of the American Academy of Political and Social Science,* May, 1957.

Spicer, Edward H. *Cycles of Conquest: The Impact of Spain, Mexico, and the United States on the Indians of the Southwest, 1533-1960.* Tucson: The University of Arizona Press, 1962.

Spicer, Edward H. *A Short History of the Indians of the United States.* New York: Van Nostrand Reinhold Company, 1969.

CHAPTER 7

Cohen, Felix S. "How Long Will Indian Constitutions Last?" *Indians At Work,* vol. 6, no. 10, 1939.

Cohen, Felix S. "Original Indian Title to Land." *Harvard Law Review,* vol. 69, p. 147, 1955.

Crosse, Murray L. "Criminal and Civil Jurisdiction in Indian Country." *Arizona Law Review,* vol. 4, no. 1, pp. 57-64, 1962.

Price, Monroe. "Law and the Social Order." *Arizona State Law Journal,* vol. 2, p. 161, 1969.

Smith, Michael. "Tribal Sovereignty and the 1968 Indian Bill of Rights." U.S. Commission on Civil Rights, *The Civil Rights Digest,* Washington, D.C., Summer, 1970.

CHAPTERS 8, 9

Brophy, William A. and Sophie D. Aberle. "The Indian: America's Unfinished Business." *The Civilization of the American Indian Series,* no. 83, Norman: University of Oklahoma Press.

Cahn, Edgar. *Our Brother's Keeper: The Indian in White America*. New York: New Community Press, World Publishing Company, 1969.

Hough, Henry W. *Development of Indian Resources*. Denver: World Press, Inc., 1967.

Lurie, Nancy O. and Stuart Levine, ed. *The American Indian Today*. Deland, Florida: Everett/Edwards, Inc., 1968.

Taylor, Benjamin J. and Dennis J. O'Connor. *Indian Manpower Resources in the Southwest: A Pilot Study*. Bureau of Business and Economic Research College of Business Administration, Arizona State University, Tempe, Arizona, 1969.

CHAPTER 10

Berry, B. *The Education of American Indians: A Survey of the Literature*. Washington, D.C.: U. S. Government Printing Office, 1969.

Havighurst, Robert J. *The Education of Indian Children and Youth*. Center for Urban and Regional Affairs, University of Minnesota, 1970.

Officer, J. E. *Indians in School*. Bureau of Ethnic Research, University of Arizona, Tucson, 1956.

Index

165